BEST OF

Blue Ridge

DINNERWARE

IDENTIFICATION
&
VALUE GUIDE

Betty & Bill Newbound

COLLECTOR BOOKS
A Division of Schroeder Publishing Co., Inc.

FRONT COVER: Top left: Daniel Boone character jug; lower left: Indian character jug; center: quail plate; right: bud vase

Cover design by Beth Summers

Book design by Heather Warren

COLLECTOR BOOKS
P.O. Box 3009
Paducah, Kentucky 42002-3009

www.collectorbooks.com

Copyright © 2003 Betty and Bill Newbound

The current values in this book should be used only as a guide. They are not intended to set prices, which vary from one section of the country to another. Auction prices as well as dealer prices vary greatly and are affected by condition as well as demand. Neither the authors nor the publisher assumes responsibility for any losses that might be incurred as a result of consulting this guide.

Searching For A Publisher?

We are always looking for people knowledgeable within their fields. If you feel that there is a real need for a book on your collectible subject and have a large comprehensive collection, contact Collector Books.

Contents

Dedication and Thanks

This book is dedicated to, first of all, Norma and Sherman Lilly, our helpers and stalwart friends of almost 25 years. Also our sincere thanks to Don and Susan Burkett, Jay Parker, and Kent Lee for all the time and effort spent helping with the pictures for this volume. We couldn't have done it without you! Last but far from least, to all the collectors country wide who have always been so kind, supportive, and willing to share information, pictures, and stories. We love you all!

In addition, a loving thank you to our daughter, Emalee, who not only taught Mom about the dreaded computer, but even did a share of the typing herself! Thank you, thank you, Honey!

Best Bets for Friends and Help

The National Blue Ridge Newsletter
Norma Lilly
144 Highland Drive
Blountville, TN 37617
6 issues per year

4

History of Blue Ridge Dinnerware

In 1917, Erwin, Tennessee, was a typical small southern town, going about its own quiet business. But the winds of change were about to blow through, as they always do, and life there would never be the same.

At the turn of the century, America's railroads could not survive by depending solely on carrying freight and passengers from here to there. Industries must be developed along the railroad lines to ensure future business. Since the white kaolin clay and feldspar necessary to pottery making was available close to Erwin, the Carolina, Clinchfield, and Ohio Railroad's Halston Corporation sold land to E. J. Owens and his son, Ted, for the purpose of building a pottery. Mr. Owens had been associated with Owens China Company in Ohio.

By 1918, the pottery had been built along with about forty company houses. Several dozen skilled pottery workers and their families were imported from the areas of East Liverpool and Sebring, Ohio, and Chester, West Virginia. Traditional decal decorated and gold-trimmed chinaware was produced under the name Clinchfield Pottery. In 1920, a charter was issued with the name Southern Potteries, Inc.

This traditional dinnerware enjoyed only a mild success and after a couple of years, the Erwin plant was purchased by Charles W. Foreman who had been associated with Owens in the aforementioned Owens China Company. George F. Brandt was brought to Erwin as plant manager.

Mr. Foreman brought with him the technique of hand painting under the glaze, and this revolutionized Southern Potteries. Girls and women from the hills applied for work at Southern Potteries, were trained in the free-hand painting technique, and began work. This technique with its spectrum of bright colors and uninhibited approach was a welcome innovation in the world of decal-decorated dinnerware and an instant success. By 1938, Southern had evolved to a full hand-painting operation and "Blue Ridge, Hand-painted Under the Glaze" dinnerware was well established.

A large national sales organization was maintained with showrooms in a number of large cities such as Chicago and New York City. Along with this modern upscale merchandising were the small mom & pop stores who often received their Blue Ridge orders from a traveling man with a pickup truck carrying dinnerware classed as "seconds" and even "thirds."

With the onset of World War II, imported chinaware was cut off and Southern Potteries expanded enormously. During the peak productions years of the 1940s and early 1950s, workers numbered over one thousand and more than 324,000 pieces of decorated ware were produced each week! This made Southern Potteries Blue Ridge the leading dishware line in the nation.

By the mid-1950s, the war was over and imports were again flooding the market. The cost of labor was rising and competition from other potteries and the new plastic dinnerware was fierce. Despite all efforts to stay afloat, on January 31, 1957, an *Erwin Record* extra edition headline read "Southern Potteries Stockholders Vote to Close Plant." This liquidation marked the end of over 40 years of production of one of the nation's most original and attractive dinnerwares. The closing hit Erwin hard because the majority of employed folk in the town worked in some capacity or other at either the pottery or the railroad.

Only a small part of the old pottery building remains today. The company houses have long since been sold, remodeled, and blended into the town. Many of Southern's mold cases (the master forms from which molds are made), were purchased by Ray and Pauline Cash, owners of Clinchfield Artware Pottery and remained in use for many years. It was truly the end of an era, and Erwin will always remember the great days when Southern Potteries was the best in the nation.

The Potters

While you're admiring your beautiful Blue Ridge pieces, take a minute or two to consider how much work went into making each and every piece. For instance, in making just a simple plate, a man known as the batterout took a handful of clay and plopped it down on a plaster of Paris block with a domed face on it. Then he picked up a 26 pound second block with handles on the sides and hit the lump of clay just right to make a pancake. This was then peeled off and put on another block for the jiggerman to continue the job. Since a good jiggerman could form an unbelievable 55 to 60 dozen plates an

hour, you can see how much weight that poor batterout had to lift in a day! After a few years, the process became more mechanized and was not quite so hard physically.

Cups were formed in a mold which shaped the outside, while at the same time, a hand tool was used for inside shaping. Handles were molded on a "tree" and while still leathery and pliable, they were cut away with a knife whose blade was curved to match the outside of the cup. They were attached with a slip that formed a sort of glue. After that, the cup had to be re-shaped on a spinning block by a man called a turner. Turners received $6.35 per hundred dozen cups!

The next steps were the first kiln firing for bisque, then the decorating, then applying the glaze, another firing and a visit to the finishing department where any protrusions were knocked off with a piece of steel held in the hand. Since the glaze actually turns to glass, this was another fairly dangerous job. The flying glass was really amazing and one needed protection for the eyes. Inspection and sorting came next and then warehousing and shipping.

In the early years, Southern Potteries made its own barrels for shipping, gathered the straw for packing, and put together the sectioned paper shipping containers used later on. Haulers would pull up their trucks, large and small, and load up with dinnerware. Some 425,000 pieces a week went everywhere from major department stores to little mom and pop dime stores throughout the country.

The decorating department was sometimes called the heart and soul of the pottery. If so, then the potters, turners, finishers etc. were the strength and determination that helped make Blue Ridge America's leading hand-painted dinnerware for over 40 years.

The Decorators

Imagine 500 girls in a huge, bright room under a sawtooth roof, talking, laughing, dishes clashing, brushes flying. This was the decorating shop — the heart and soul of the pottery. Here the colorful and sometimes fantastic flowers, fruits, and birds that collectors today love, first came into being.

When a person was hired into the decorating department, the foreman would take a group and teach them the basic strokes of folk painting. Some were talented, some were not, but they were given simple patterns to copy and many started work the same day. They would join a crew of two to four girls who each concentrated on a certain part of the pattern, some doing leaves, some buds or petals, etc. Jobs were changed frequently to avoid monotony and keep a fresh approach. Most patterns were done purely freehand which accounts for the fascinating little changes we find when a number of plates of the same pattern are displayed together. Here is a bud that is not repeated on its sister plate — or one leaf instead of two. Or perhaps the flowers are larger on one plate than on another. Sometimes a girl would add a little personal squiggle to a flower, marking it as her work. All these little differences contribute to the charm

that makes this handwork so appealing to collectors today.

The most talented painters moved on to the intricate porcelain ware pieces where each girl painted an entire piece from start to finish. During the mid-1940s, a few of the very best decorators were selected to do a limited number of scenic and wildlife plates and large platters. They are signed with the artist's name on the lower right hand edge of the painting. I understand some of the best painters could do five or six of the artist-signed turkey platters in one day!

Almost all of the hundreds of patterns used originated at the plant. The chief designer, Lena Watts, was a native of Erwin. She was not a professional artist — just a girl with a flair for design, a feeling for color, and a love of nature. Her scenic plates depicting lonely cabins, mills, and the various wildlife scenes and huge turkey platters are indeed fine examples of folk art. In later years, Lena moved to Stetson China Company, which explains the similarity between some Stetson patterns and Blue Ridge. Lena's place at Southern was filled by Rosmae Rowland, who held the position until Southern's closing in 1957.

Shape Up!

How do you identify the maker of a piece of china when there's no mark and the pattern is unfamiliar or unassuming? By the shape, of course! By the molded pattern on the edge of a plate or the shape of the handle on a cup or the body shape of a sugar bowl or gravy boat. Shape is what it's all about. More than color, more than style — shape tells the story.

There were twelve basic shapes made in the everyday dinnerware. They are

Astor	Skyline
Candlewick	Skyline Studioware
Clinchfield	Trailway
Colonial	Trellis
Palisades	Waffle
Piecrust	Woodcrest

Other shapes you may find are

Cake plates
Curlique Arches
Lotus Leaf
Lace Edge

Keep in mind that patterns did not always appear on the same shape.

Astor, narrow, slightly cupped edge

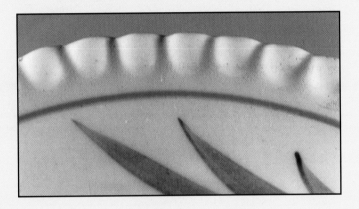

Candlewick, beaded edge

Clinchfield, wide, flat rim

Colonial, fluted edge

Piecrust, crimped edge, introduced 1948

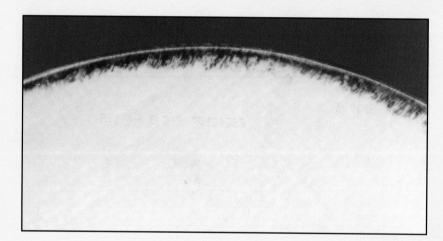

Woodcrest, textured surface, called "burlap" by workers, because that was what lined the molds.

Trellis border of vertically fluted spaces between which are areas of cross-hatching

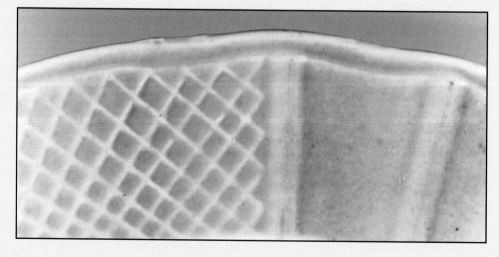

Lotus

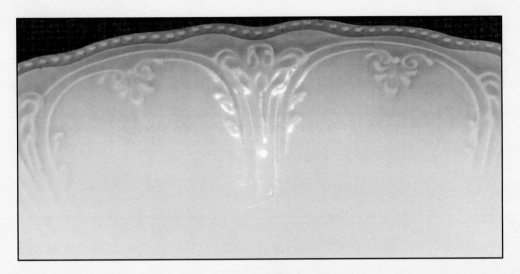

Curlique Arches

Early bowl shape

Cake plate

"Scattered Leaves" (L), "Bachelor Buttons" (R)

"Mistress Mary"

"Ship Ahoy"

"Johnny Appleseed"

"Jonquil" (L), "Memory Lane" (R)

"Mary" (setting)

"Kitchen Shelf" (L), "Fluffy Ruffles" (R)

"Tweeting Trio"

"Teal Roseanna" (L), "Solitaire" (R)

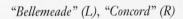

"Burro" legend says "Dear Judge: The Old Mule is Still in the Ring but Badly Bent." Signed C.W.F. April 15, 1941

"Bellemeade" (L), "Concord" (R)

"Blossom Time" (L), "Vineyard" (R)

"Bristol Bouquet" (L),
"Roanoke" (R)

"Recollection" (L), "Tara" (R)

"Golden Jubilee" (L), "Spring Shower" (R)

"Bug-a-Boo" (L), "Sonora" (R)

"Snippet" breakfast in bed set

"October" breakfast set

"Hopscotch" (L), "Kingsport" (R)

"Eglantine" (L), "Calais" (C), "Primrose Path" (R)

"Beggarweed" (L), "English Garden" (R)

"Beverly" (L), "Folk Art Fruit" (R)

"Love Song" (L), "Picardy" (R)

"Pansy" (L), "Flowering Branch" (R)

"Zachary"   *"Tweet"*

"Fetching" (L), "Threesome" (R)

"Winner's Circle" (L), "Blackberry" (R)

"Tulip Circle" (L), "Prima Donna" (R)

"Mary's Garden" (L), Barbara's Bouquet (R)

"Lass Linda" (L), "Marjorie" (R)

"Beauty Secret" (L), "Freedom Ring" (R)

"Greenfeather" (L), "Three Sisters" (R)

"Miss Piggy" (L), "Sailboat" (R)

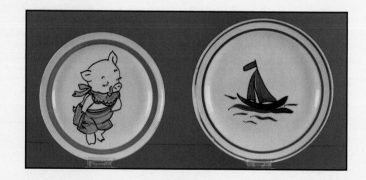

"Sonora" (two on L), "Mexico Lindo" (C), "Mexicano" (R)

"Calais"

"Abby Rose"

"Somerset" (L), "Scuppernog" (R)

"Moe's Cabin"

"Nonsense"

"Johnson City" (L), "Floral Medley" (R)

"Mary Jeanne" (L), "Carmellia" (R)

"Sydney's Hope"

"Purple Passion"

"Sue-Lynn"

"Wildlings"

"Riotous"

"Fern Tulip" (L), "Fraktur" (R)

"Chatelaine"

"Balsam Poplar" (also in Waffle)

"Song Sung Blue"

"Brittany" set

"Cock o' the Walk" (L), "Grape Salad" (R)

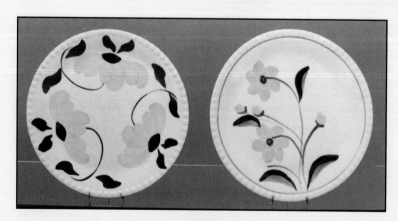

"Sundance" (L) "Sunshine" (R)

"Rockport Rooster" (L), "Think Pink" (R)

"Tame Strawberry" (L), "Lone Apple" (R)

"Mitchell Iris" (L), "Trousseau" (R)

"California Poppy" (L), "Rooster Motto" (C), "Callaway," Piecrust (R)

"Aurora" (L), "Glorious" (R)

Quaker Apple (L), "Fayette Fruit" (R)

Mountain Rose (L), "Vixen" (R)

"Sundowner" (L), "Full Bloom" (R)

"Cocky-Locky" set

"Spindrift" (L), "Confetti" (R)

*"Mariner" (L), "Tulip Trio" (R)
(also found in other color combinations)*

"Brownie" (L), "Brunswick" (R)

"Heirloom" (L), "Bristol Lily" (R)

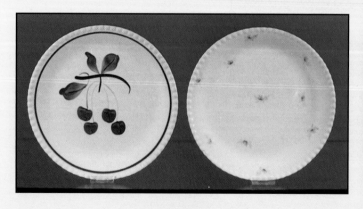

"Quartet" (L), "Rosebud" (R)

"Michelle"

"Mary" set

"Richard" (L), "Waverly" (R)

"Flirtation" (L), "Adoration" (R)

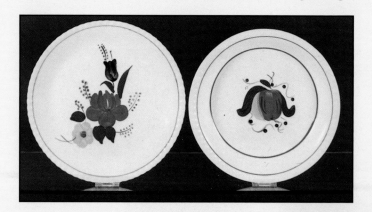

"Harmony" (L), "Peachy" (R)

"Around Rosey" (L), "Firecracker" (R)

"Pastel Leaf" (L), "Sunshine Variant" (R)

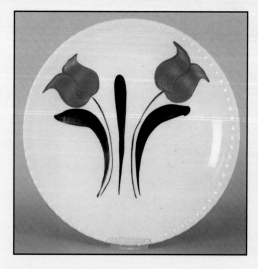

"Ochoee"

"Seedlings"

Ham 'N Eggs set   *"Patty Cake"*

"Louisiana Lace" (Hester) (L), "Christmas Ornament" (R)

"Country Road Variant" (L), "Tricolor" (R)

"Willoberry" (L), "Blue Moon" (R)

"Grass Flower"   *"Black-eyed Susan"*

"Starflower" (L), "Russellville" (R)

"Lizzie's Gift"

"Kelvin"

"Dana's Garden"

"First Smoke"

"Golden Rays," signed D. HUPP on back

"Ship Ahoy"

"Maple Leaf Rag"

"Alexandria" (L), "Ledford" (R)

"Rosemary" (L), "Twin Flowers" (R)

"Wilshire," all silver stamped, see marks section

"Whirl"

"Wytheville," advertising

"Evelyn"

"Timothy"

"Bird Dog" (L), "Big Catch" (C) (also in blue on Clinchfield), "Fala" (R), 11½"

"Lyonnaise"

"General McArthur"

"Black Cocker" (L),
"Spaniel" (C), "Spaniel"
square plate (R)

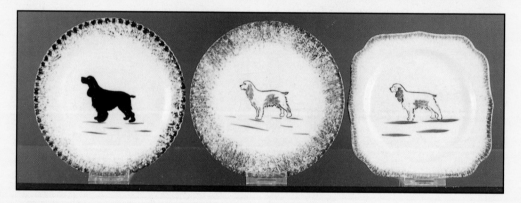

"Mowing Hay" (L), Candlewick
shape, "Watering the Flowers"
(R), Skyline from Provincial
Farm Series

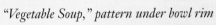

"Vegetable Soup," pattern under bowl rim

"Vegetable Soup" salad bowl & underplate

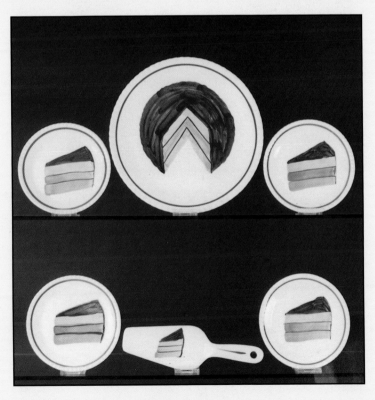

"Piece of Cake" set

"Windsong"

"Gerbera"

"Miss Annie" (L), "Triple Crown," Waffle shape (R)

"Fox Grape" 17" platter

"Gale"

"Fighting Cocks"

"Lyonnaise"

"Picardy"

"Veronica" (L), "Brittany" (R)

"Teardrops & Roses" (L), "Spring Fever" (R)

"Entwined"

"Fruit Ring"

"Spring Song" set

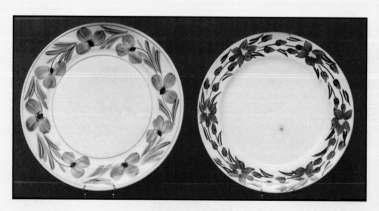

"Unicoi" (L), "Red Queen" (R)

"Big Catch"

"Do-Si-Do"

"Leaf Ring" (L), "Hex Sign" (R)

"Fairmede Fruits" (L),
"Ruby" (R)

Ice Maiden

"Bluecurls" (L), "Rehoboth" (R)

"Kaleidoscope"

"Abracadabra" (L), "Mosaic" (R)

"Tintagel"

"Dragon Song" (L) Astor, "Fanciful" (R)

"Floral Spray" (L), "Apple Tart" (R)

"Mountain Daisy"

"Perfection" (L), "PinkTulip" (R)

"Delectible" (L), "Dutch Red" (R)

"Windjammer" (L), "Cocky-Locky" (R)

"Peony"

"Brittany" set

"Thanksgiving Turkey on Sand"

"Red Leaf" (L), "Border Print"

"Erin" (L), "Hula Bowl" (R)

"Tansy" (L), "Feliciana" (R)

"Gamecock" (L), "Winery" (R)

"Rowdy"

"Ellie's Place"

"Shannon"

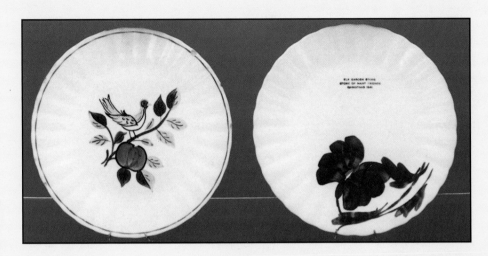

Yorktown (L) (Talisman pattern),
Blue Flower (R)

"Snappy" (L), "Clairborne" (R)

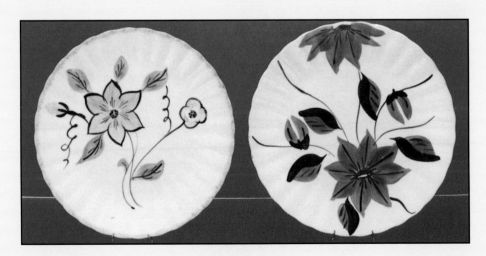

"Lexington" (L), "Orion" (R)

"Verona" (L), "Autumn Laurel" (R)

"Strathmoor" (L), "Carol's Roses" (R)

"Pink Petticoat" (L), "Amhurst" (R)

"Stardancer" (L), "Carlile" (R)

"Fox Grape" (L), "Rose Hill" (R)

"Becky" (L), "Nocturne" (R)

"Sunbright" (L), "Bluefield" (R)

"Rose Hill" pieces

"Teacher's Pet"

"Mistress Mary" pieces

"Chickory" pieces

"Whirligig"

"Rainelle" (L), "Pembrooke" (R)

"Iris Anne" (L), "Cherish" (R)

"County Fair" chop plate (L),
"Tickled Pink" (R)

"Alleghany" (L), "Pristine" (R)

"Beth" (L), "Remembrance" (R)

Polka Dot

"Flower Bowl" (L), "Joanna" (R)

"Medley" (L), "Kate" (R)

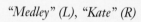

"Champagne Pinks" (L), "Hornbeak" (R)

"Wildwood Flower" (L), "Savannah" (R)

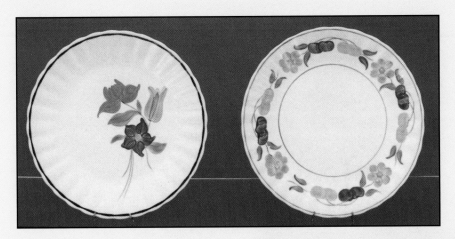

"Potpourri" (L), "Cherry Blossom" (R)

"Roxalana" (L), "Pansy Trio" (R)

Fruit Fantasy pieces

"Chintz" pieces

Chrysanthemum pieces

"Fox Grape" pieces

"Wild Strawberry" pieces

"Dreambirds" pieces

"Flower Bowl" selection

"Little Red Head"

Selection of portrait plates; left to right: "Cpl. Edw. S. Guinn, 34235489, Btry B, 579th AAA, GWBA (SP), c/o Postmaster APO 18657 San Francisco, Calif; "Vergie & Sherrell"; small plate, "Pvt. Mitchell Williams, U.S. Army, Fort Bragg, NC May 14, 1943, All my love, Mary"; Soldier plate "Love" then, "Corporal Mitchell Williams, USA"; no writing

Yorktown (L), Cup: Blossom Tree, Cherry Time (R) (Talisman pieces)

Talisman Wild Strawberry

"Rechan-a-la-Mode" edge variation

"French Peasant"

"Mountain Empire"

"Orleans"

"Calypso" (L), "Dewberry" (R)

"Wrinkled Rose" (L),
"Shenandoah" (R)

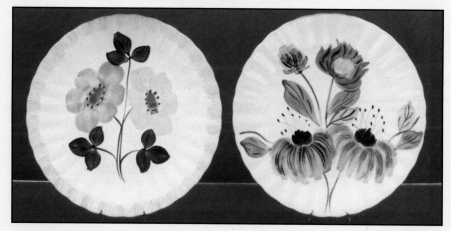

"Crystal" (L), "LeShay" (R)

"Christine" (L), "Chatam" (R)

"Taffeta" (L), "Grape Harvest" (R)

"Kibler's Rose" (L), "Annalee" (R)

"Farmer Takes a Wife"

Ashley's Bouquet cup, saucer, demi tray

"Crew Ninety-two," signed by members and dated 1944

"Our Lisa"

"Petite Point"

"Alex and Vicki"

"Millie's Bouquet"

"Burkett's Garden"

"Candace" (L) also on Palisades, "Rose Camellia" (R)

"Backyard Bleeding Heart"

"Tempo" (L), "Camelot" (R)

"Reflection" (L), "Floribunda" (R)

"Folklore" (L) Woodcrest,
"Cherry Tree Glen" (R)

"Jingle Bell Poinsettia"

"Cabbage Rose"

"Claremont" (L), "Trumpet Vine" (R)

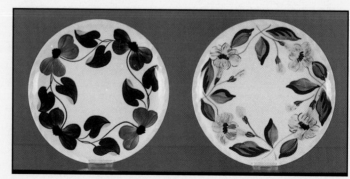

"Teal Roseanna" (L), "Sweetheart" (R)

"Willow" (L), "Plum Nelly" (R), Plum out of Tennessee, and Nelly out of Georgia

"Spring Blossom"

"Bounteous"

"Velma"　　　　　　　　　　*"Boutonniere"*

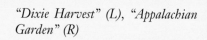
"Dixie Harvest" (L), "Appalachian Garden" (R)

"Wanda's Wild Rose" (L), "Mazurka" (R)

"Aragon" (L), "Hillside" (R)

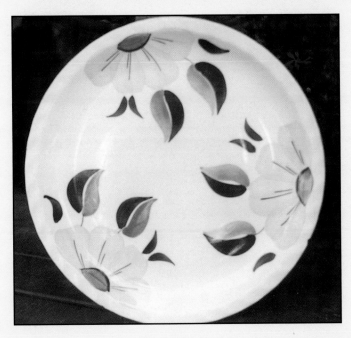

"Rise 'n Shine"

"Emlyn"

"Lauren" (L), "Southern Special" (R)

"Square Dancers" (L), "Freedom" (R)

Apple Blossom

Marking on above

"Ridge Harvest" (L), "Cherry Wine" (R)

"Spring Morning" (L), "Kibler" (R)

"Whipstitch"

Spring Morning (Ruffin)

"Donegal"

"Chicken Little," Piecrust sugar

Piecrust sugar lid

"Cadenza" (L), "Flirt" (R)

"Ralph's Orchard"

"The Caller," Square Dance set

"Covered Bridge"

"Madelyn"

"Piedmont Plaid"

"Jessamine" (L), "Whirligig" (R)

"Hard Candy"

"Blessings," says "Blessings on our Mortgaged Home"

"Strawberry Plant"

"Apple Yard" (L), "Aqua Leaf" (R)

"Pizzicato"

"Carolina Allspice"

"Lotus" (L), "Homeplace" (R)

"Black Ming" (L), "Raz-
zle Dazzle" (R)

"Lola Faye" boxed set

"Marion"

"Chloe" (L), "Spring Mills" (R)

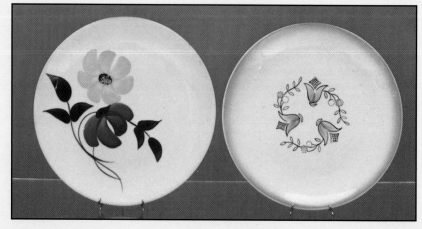

"Midas Touch" (L), "Windmill" (R)

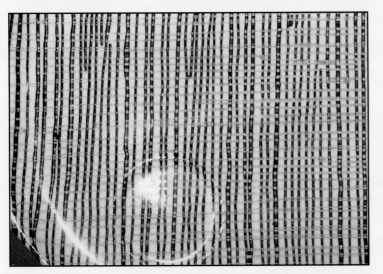

"Dalton Levi" close up

"Dusty Miller"

"Briarwood" (L), "Tea Rose" (R)

"Flight"

"Homestead"

"Gloriosa" (L), "Berry Patch" (R)

"Leaf Spray" (L), "Slim Pickins" (R)

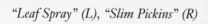

"Wishing Well" (L), "Red Rooster" (R)

"Serenade" (L), "Greencastle" (R)

"Under the Sea"

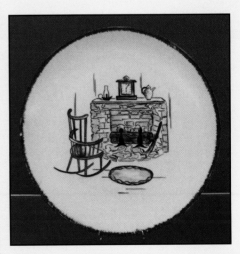

"Fireside"

"Blackbirds" (L), "Isobel" (R)

"Indian Summer"

"Alvin"

"Vegetable Patch" (L), "Farmyard" (R)

"Bonsai" (L), "Meadowlea" (R)

"Buck a Rooster"

"Cherry Time," Talisman

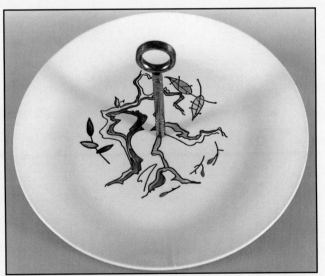

"Rocky Face"

"Windy Day," center handle

"Bardstown" (L), "Pinecone" (R)

"Flower Fantasy"

"Frageria" (L), "Granny Smith Apple" (R)

"Orchid"

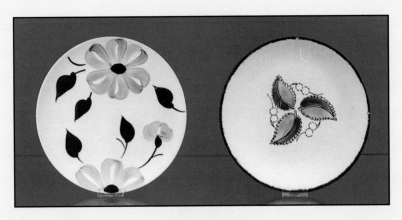

"Bowknot" (L), color variation of Whirligig, "Wild Cherry" (R)

"Normandy," man and woman

"Christmas Doorway" (L), "Feathered Friends" (R)

"Alma's Fruit Salad," signed "Alma '55" on front

"Fireglow"

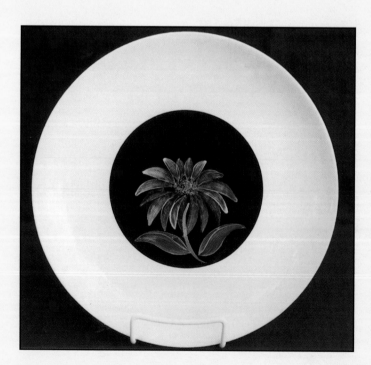

"Shady Lady"

"Rossville"

"Prelude" (L), "Sarasota" (R)

"Strawberry Sundae" (L),
"Jigsaw" (R), reproduced

"Lavalette" (L), "Bethany
Berry" (R)

"Vegetable Patch" (L), "Glory" (R)

"Smoky Mountain Cabin" (L), "Stream-side Cabin" (R)

"Robin" (L), "Nesting Birds" (R)

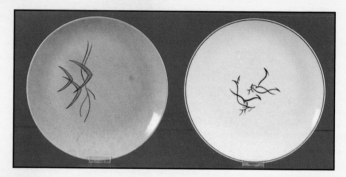

"Strawberry Duet" (L), "Bluefield" (R), also with pink

"Blackbirds"

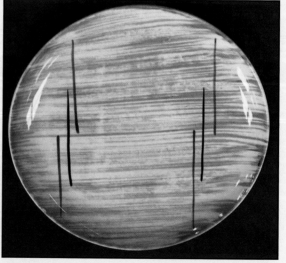

"Rainy Day"

"Margaret Rose" (L), "Woodbine" (R)

"Street's Barnyard"

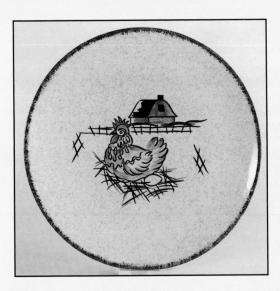

"Chicken Feed"

Pa #1 mark

Hen #1 mark

"Normandy"

"Butterfly Bouquet"

"Cock 'o the Morning," Rooster and Hen shakers (various colors)

"Le Coq"

"Le Coq Soleil"

"Sanctuary," on back: initials "V.H." for Vickie (Hensley) Ledford

Trailway

"Leaves of Fall"

"Country Fruit" (L), "Thistle" (R)

"Gingham Fruit" (L), "Cock-a-Doodle" (R)

Trellis

"Nature Trail"

"Sweet Rocket" (L), "Maple Leaf" (R)

"Stencil" (L), "Exotic" (R)

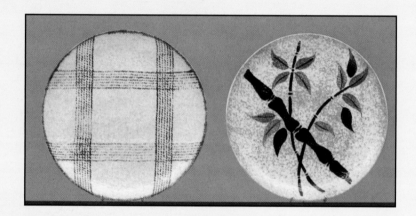

"Pleasant Acres" (L), "Quilted Fruit" (R)

Eventide

"Quilted Fruit" soup

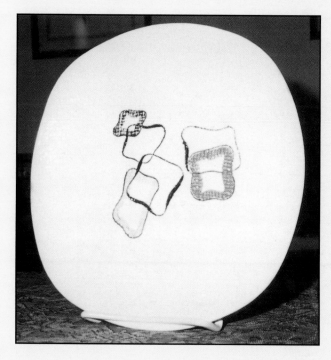

"Square Meal"

"Marlene"

"Little 'Uns" party set

"Roses Are Red"

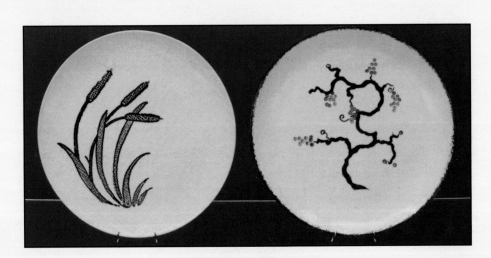

"Caretta Cattail" (L), "Ming Blossom" (R)

"Patchwork"

"Black Bottom" (L), "Needlepoint Fruit" (R)

"Abingdon" (L), "Stitchery" (R)

"Hawaiian Ti" (L), "Cheston" (R)

"Cross Patch" (L), "Swinnett" (R)

"Belle Haven"

April

Samples

When the head designer at Southern Potteries created a pattern, she had to keep track of the number of colors used and the number of brush strokes necessary to complete it. Often the names of the colors will be shown on the sample piece, along with the pattern number. Remember, Southern Potteries only used pattern numbers, not names, unless the pattern was nationally advertised. After a few pieces were finished, the piece was submitted to the management who would consider the cost of the paint and the number of man hours (or in this case, woman hours) needed. If they decided the pattern could be made at a profit, the approved stamp was applied and a place setting or two were made to exhibit at the big dinnerware shows or to show visiting buyers. Sometimes a pattern did not sell and was quickly discontinued with the display pieces sold as seconds. This results in collectors finding a plate or two for a certain pattern and never finding another piece. Today, collectors snap up the sample-marked pieces as fast as they can as they make a very interesting addition to any collection.

"Allene," painted by Allene Miller

"Chloe"

"Serenade"

"Tea Rose"

"Maidenpink"

"Lass Linda"

"Apple Pan Dowdy" vegetable bowl

"Nola" (L), "Nocturne" (R)

"Likeness" (L), "Country Strawberry" (R)

Quarter-pound butter dish

"Nesting Birds"

Paint sample plate, B.R. Drakenfeld liquid underglaze colors

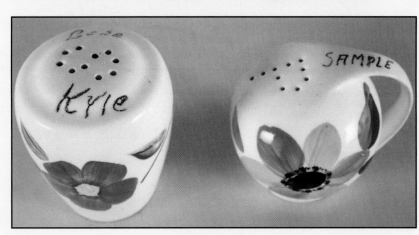

Skyline shakers

Miscellaneous Shapes

"Devilish," Fish Scale shape

"Bunny Tails," Fish Scale shape

"Garden Wedding" (L), "Dreamy" (R)

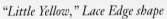

"Little Yellow," Lace Edge shape

"Best in Show," Lace Edge shape

Top, left to right: "Heart Throb" pitcher and shakers, "Shadow Fruit" pitcher, Palisades; Bottom, "Heart Throb" bowl, "Water Flower" gravy, Palisades shape

"Shimmer," Palisades shape

Southern Rose, Wide Rib shape

"Daffy," Fine Rib shape

"Glenda" (L), "Daisy Chain" (R), Squared Rib shape

"Holly Wreath," Waffle shape

"Celina"

"Midsummer Rose," Waffle shape

"Pauline" cake plate

"Cross Stitch" divided plate, "Butterfly & Leaves," Trellis shape

"Gumdrop Wreath" cake plate

"Julie" pie baker, "Dreambirds" platter, Colonial shape

Artist Palette advertising plates. Talisman Wallpaper plate (L) Blue Ridge (R). In 1950 – 52, United Wallpaper Co., decided to coordinate wallpaper with Blue Ridge china. The idea was not successful and few were made.

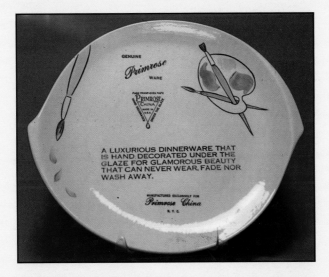

Artist Palette advertising Primrose China Co., a jobber for Blue Ridge

Square Shapes

"Brilliance" (L), "First Love" (R), rounded squares

"Twirl," Old Clinchfield mark

"Granite," pink and gray

"Zinnia" (L), "Festoon" (R)

"Tapestry," Old Clinchfield mark   *"Eileen," Old Clinchfield mark*

"Fiddlesticks" (L), "Déjà Vu"
(R), rounded squares

"Tennessee Mule," profile   *"Tennessee Mule," full face*

"Green Grapes"

"Cheers" plates, one is painted in corner with red arches, other on side with no arches

"Gamecock," 7½" square

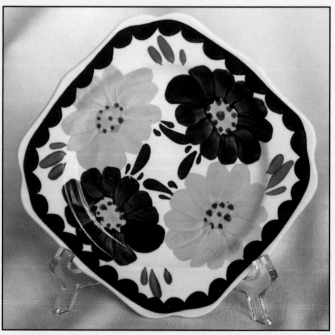

"Flashy," PV mark

"Weathervane," PV mark, Blue Ridge

Weathervane made in France, marked "Min Village" not Blue Ridge

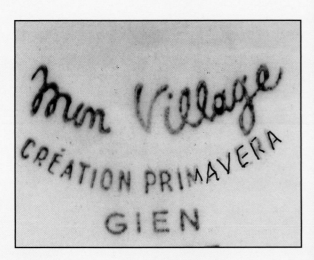

Min Village mark

"Josey's Posies"

"Chickory" (L) "Minty" (R)

Cup and Gravy Shapes

Top: Trailway, rope handle, (L), Trellis (C), Woodcrest (R); Bottom: Square handle (L), Skyline, (C), Astor (R)

Top: Colonial (L), "Turkey with Acorns" cup (R); Bottom: Candlewick (L), Piecrust (R)

Woodcrest cup, note square base

"Arleen" heavy demi cup and saucer

Trellis cup and saucer

Regular demi cup and saucer

Children's mugs: "Red Star," "Stardancer," "Lyonnaise"

Both sides of Skyline "Christmas Doorway" cup

Jumbo cup, "Bulldog" pattern, entire cup

"Bulldog" cup with handle removed, shows slot where handle attaches

Regular Jumbo cup and saucer in "Timothy" pattern

Jumbo cup and saucer (Father also)

Demi cup, saucer and tray, "Nove Rose"

Top: "Hops with Bow," Trailway (L); "Vignette," Skyline (R); center: "Sundance Variant," Candlewick, (L); "North Star Cherry," Colonial (R); bottom: Green Briar, Piecrust (L); "Red Carpet," Astor (R)

"Red Bank" two spout gravy on attached tray, only one we've seen!

Vegetable Bowl Shapes

Piecrust "Spring Morning," Candlewick "Around Rosey"

Colonial "French Peasant"

Colonial "Chintz," edge appears plain with lid

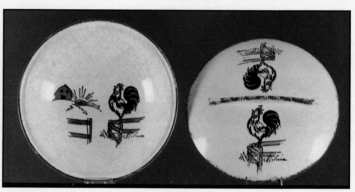

Skyline "Cock 'o the Morning," very difficult to hold handle

"Dungannon" covered vegetable

Colonial "Elegance"

Clinchfield "Leaf" color variation

Poinsettia pieces apart, note lovely pattern in bottom of dish

Poinsettia with lid

"Red Bank" open vegetable with wavy center divider

Miscellaneous Hollow Ware

"French Peasant" covered toast, lady on lid, gentleman on plate

"French Peasant" toast lid on round 8" plate (L), covered toast on usual square plate (R)

"Barn & Silo" coffee bottle (originally called carafe) with stand

Demi-size earthenware sugar and creamer

Center handle tray with hammered aluminum edge and center post on "Whirligig" pattern plate

"Whirligig" plate with wide hammered aluminum edge and base

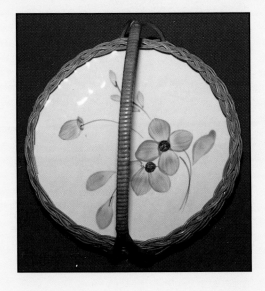

Colonial "Pfiffle" plate in basket, plate is placed inside wet wicker, which then shrinks to fit

Skyline salt and pepper

Peters Hot Chocolate crock, 8½" tall and wide, with original metal lid and ladle, probably used in a restaurant

Original metal lid and ladle for Peters Hot Chocolate crock, note Peters name on handle of ladle

A selection of salt and pepper shakers

Speckled chicks, initialed on base

"Lyonnaise" range shakers

Figurines

When collecting — or trying to collect — figurines, please keep in mind that unless the item is stamped S.P. Inc., Erwin, Tennessee, or has an authentic label, they could have been made by any number of potteries. They all copied from one another and identical figurines have turned up with the marks of various potteries. For instance, in the book *Morton Potteries — 95 Years* by Doris and Burdell Hall, the same lioness figure shown below is also on their page 107 as a product of Cliftwood Art Potteries in Morton, Illinois. Don't buy an expensive, unmarked figure just because someone says it came from the pottery.

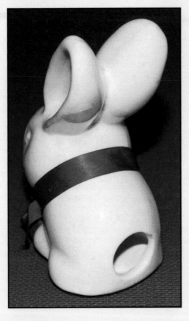

"Cottontail Rabbit" cotton ball holder

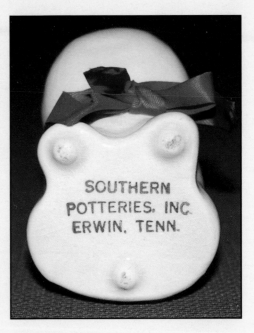

Marked base of "Cottontail Rabbit"

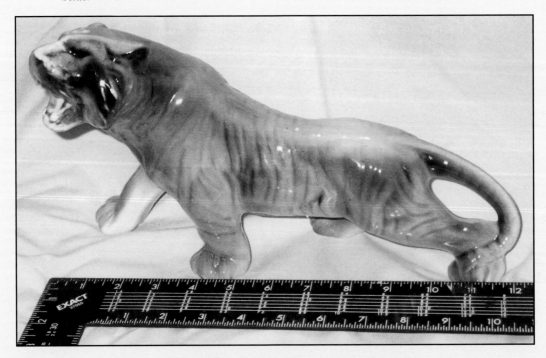

12½" Lioness figure, Southern Potteries sticker on tummy

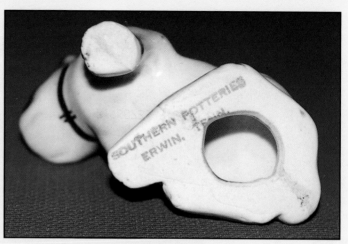

Gold ink marks on dog figure

Dog figure, 3½" tall, stamped on back BPWL, Erwin, TN

Art Nouveau nude figures, both marked on base, 6½" and 8½" tall

Miscellaneous Trays

We're showing a number of gravy and other small trays because so often the pattern on the tray is only a part of the entire pattern used on plates, making the little trays difficult to identify.

"Beaded Apple" gravy tray

"Grandmother's Garden" gravy tray

"Wild Strawberry" gravy tray

"Mardi Gras" gravy tray

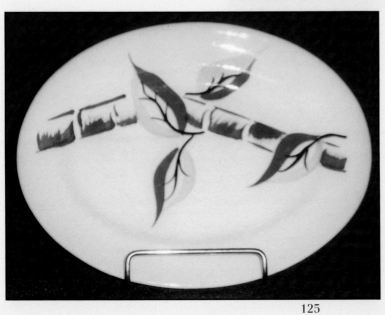

"Sarasota" gravy tray

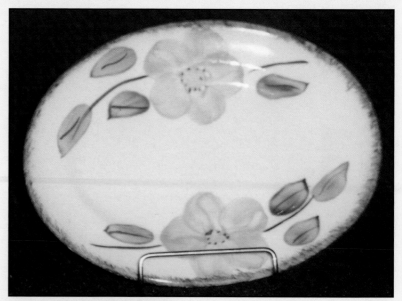

"Prairie Rose" gravy tray

"Wild Cherry #3" gravy tray

"Blue Bell Bouquet" gravy tray

"Spring Hill Tulip" gravy tray

"Chintz" gravy tray

"Willa" gravy tray

"Red Ring" gravy tray

"Hawaiian Fruit" gravy tray

"Pom Pom" gravy tray

"Red Bank" waffle set tray

"Chintz" oval relish tray

"French Peasant" Skyline demi tray with lady only (L), same on Colonial blank with woman only

"Tiger Lily" demi tray

Salad and Dessert Plates

Sets of usually eight plates, mainly 8½" in size, were loved by the "Ladies that lunch," and are known as salad sets. They held a generous serving of salad with perhaps a roll alongside.

We're including the Square Dancers set in this category. Mainly because of the size of the squared plates and the fact that with them came a large 12" salad bowl and a 14" underplate. Also in this pattern, however, came round party plates with cup wells and cups, all on Piecrust shape. There is also a coffee bottle in this pattern.

Smaller plates, usually square and around 6" in diameter were used as dessert sets. (Bill says they're not big enough for *his* dessert!)

Today, we find sets gracing collectors' walls, especially the lovely Songbird sets and the more exotic Carribean and Mandarin sets.

Mandarin set, "Pomegranate"

"Square Dancers" set, party plates with cup wells and salad bowls. Notice that cups all carry the same pattern while plates are all different.

Mandarin set, "Chinese Junk"

Mandarin set, "Pagodas"

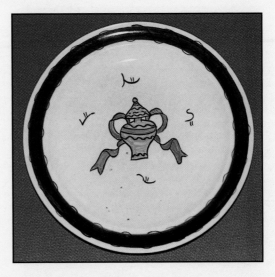

Mandarin set, "Temple Jar"

Mandarin set, "Scroll"

Mandarin set, "Blue Bottle Gourd"

Mandarin set, "Plum Blossom"

Mandarin set, "Shield"

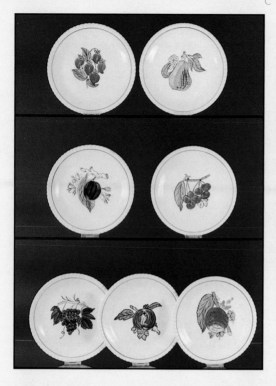

"Fruited Plain" plate number eight

"Fruited Plain" set, Candlewick, seven plates shown of eight

"Fruited Plain" 11½" underplate

"Fruited Plain" 10" salad bowl

"Le Coq Soleil" salad bowl and four plates on Skyline shape

"Fruit Cocktail" set on Astor shape

"Phyllis L" set on Astor shape

"County Fair" set on Colonial, four shown

"County Fair" set on Colonial, four shown. In 1941, Avon gave a set of eight to salespeople who sent in a single order of $150.00 or more. The sets sold retail in 1942 for $3.75.

"Garden Flowers" set on Colonial shape; top, left to right: Kansas Gayfeather, Red Cone Flower; Hollyhock; center, left to right: Lavender Iris, Yellow Pansy, Blue Morning Glory; bottom, left to right: Yellow Mums, Single Poinsettia

"Language of Flowers" set on Candlewick shape. Top, left to right: "Do you really love me?" "You have upset (shaken) my heart. Will you come dance at the ball?; center, left to right: You are conquering (ravishing), "I adore you." "I Don't give my confidence easily."; bottom left to right: "All is finished" (It's over), "Do you love me a little?"

"Skyline Songbirds." Top, left to right: Yellow Shafted Flicker, Hooded Warbler, Scrub (Florida) Jay; center left to right: Ivory-billed Woodpecker, Catbird, Hummingbird; bottom left to right: Summer Tanager, Oriole

"Colonial Songbirds." Top, left to right: Gray Kingbird, Louisiana Woodthrush, Finch; center, left to right: Tufted Titmouse, Fork-tailed Flycatcher, Western Bluebird; bottom, left to right: Old Crow, Oriole

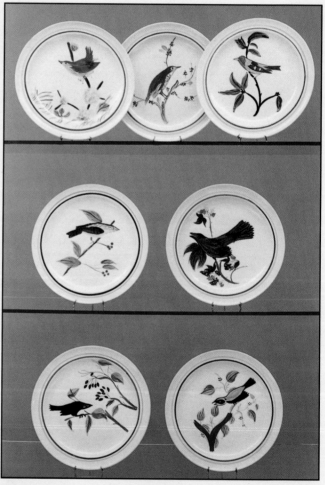

Eighth plate in "Astor Songbirds": Orchard Oriole

"Astor Songbirds." Top, left to right: Winter Wren, Hermit Thrush, Western Tanager; center, left to right: Finch, Catbird; bottom, left to right: Rusty Blackbird, Loggerhead Shrike

"Caribbean" set on Astor shape. Top, left to right: "Lemon Tree," "Sailfish," "Purkey's Paradise"; bottom, left to right: "Scenic Cruise," "Flamingo Pond," "Parrot Jungle," "Tropical Isle"

Caribbean set, eighth plate, "Carillon"

"Country Life" dessert set, 5½" six shown. Top, left to right: "Spinning Wheel," "Fisherman," "Jenny Wren"; bottom, left to right: "Grandfather Clock," "Churn," "Cradle"

Provincial Farm scenes, seven shown. Top, left to right: "Plowman," "Sowing Seed," "Harvester," "Mowing Hay"; bottom, left to right; "Watering Flowers," "Man with Pitchfork," "Flower Picker"

Mexico Lindo set, six shown. Top, left to right: "Senoritas," "Hat Dance"; bottom, left to right: "Mexican Woman," "Peanut Vender," "Cock Fights"

"Fruit Squares" set, 5¾" diameter

Happy Holidays

Thanksgiving and Christmas can surely be celebrated with our Blue Ridge holiday pattern tableware. "Turkey with Acorns" seems to be the most prolific Thanksgiving pattern, having been found in the 17½" Clinchfield platter and the 15¼" Skyline platter, plus dinner plates and cups and saucers. Notice that the cups and saucers carry only the acorn part of the pattern.

The "Thanksgiving Turkey" pattern comes in about the same composition with the 17½" platter on the Clinchfield shape and cups, saucers, and dinner plates on Skyline. Again, the cup and saucer carry only the leaf part of the design.

"Still Life" on Colonial shape features a bowl full of mouth-watering fruit to top off your dinner. Salad and/or dessert plates will be found in variations of this pattern.

A couple of plates that make nice accent pieces on your Thanksgiving table are "Turkey Surprise" and the appealing "Pilgrims," both found on Skyline shape.

Christmas patterns abound in our Blue Ridge dinnerware. First we have "Christmas Doorway" featuring an outdoor tree with some ornaments here and there. It is standing next to a welcoming doorway with a Christmas wreath decorating it. This pattern has only been found on the Skyline shape and the cups have a tree on one side and a wreath matching the one on the door on the other. This is the most elusive of the Christmas patterns.

Our indoor "Christmas Tree" pattern can be found complete with packages waiting to be opened. The 10½" plates are on the Colonial shape, as are cups and saucers. The same Christmas Tree pattern comes on a tab-handled Skyline party plate with matching cups. Christmas Tree appears to be a stamped-on and filled in with color pattern. In 1945, these sold for $5.75 for four plates!

"Christmas Tree with Mistletoe," on the Colonial shape, however, seems to have been done entirely freehand with no stamping. At first it looks like there is no star on top of this tree, but upon examining it, we find a pale yellow star that is sometimes difficult to see. There is a sprig of mistletoe to the upper right of the tree. Cups have a tree on one side and mistletoe on the other. To date, no platters have been found in these patterns.

"Hollyberry" is a great Christmas pattern with its crisp green leaves and red berries. The beautiful dinner plates, cups, and saucers are found on the Colonial shape. As so often happens in handpainted dinnerware, one of the cup and saucer sets shown has a green edge trim while the other does not. Also, the holly itself is interpreted differently on the two sets. "Hollyberry" has also been found on a tab-handled cake plate complete with lifter, a fruit bowl, and a jumbo cup.

The lovely Poinsettia pattern with its velvety red bracts can be found on the Colonial shape in many different pieces. It is sometimes also found on Skyline.

"Turkey with Acorns" 15¼" platter, Skyline, also found on 11½" Clinchfield

139

"Turkey with Acorns" table set

"Thanksgiving Turkey," Colonial shape, also shows Charlie Gibson Apple and Boyd's covered turkey dish both in glass

"Turkey with Acorns" cups and saucers, note leaves are only decorations

"Turkey Surprise," Skyline shape

"Still Life," Colonial shape

"Pilgrims," Skyline shape

"Christmas Tree with Mistletoe," Colonial shape

"Christmas Doorway"

"Christmas Tree" party set in original box

"Christmas Tree"

Poinsettia, Colonial shape

"Hollyberry" on Colonial with cups and saucers, note green edge on one and not on other

"Hollyberry" cake plate and server, jumbo cup, and fruit dish

Children's Ware

Everybody loves children's ware – cereal bowls, mugs, plates, heavy divided feeding dishes, and plates with charming animal, circus, or nursery rhyme decorations. All are avidly sought by collectors today. The several pieces of Disney-inspired children's ware are a double collectible for both Blue Ridge lovers and Disney fans. We've seen items decorated with the Three Little Pigs and Mickey Mouse.

The child's tea set is also found under this category. These were produced in various floral patterns and consisted of four each 6" plates, demi cups, demi saucers, demi pot, and demi sugar and creamer. Can you believe in the early 1950s this set sold for $5.95?

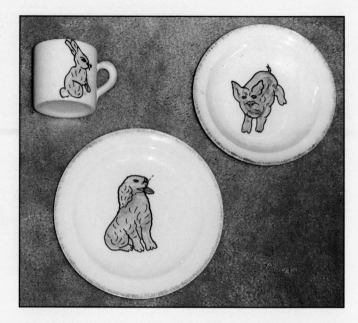

"Pink Puppy" set, Astor shape: 7" plate, 6⅜" "Blue Pig" cereal, 5oz. "Yellow Rabbit" mug. In Sears 1943 – 44 catalog this set sold for 95 cents!

"Lady Mouse," Piecrust shape

"Baby's Squirrel," Piecrust shape

"Playful Puppy," Piecrust shape

Baby's Pets, "Mother Goose," "Blue Lamb," "Piggy Blues"

"Miss Mouse," Piecrust shape

"Pig 'N Pals" set: divided bowl, "Miss Piggy" plate, "Miss Duck" cereal, "Mr. Bunny" mug, Astor shape.

"Fruit Children" child's set, Astor shape

Top: "Blue Pig" cereal, "Mama Goose," Astor shape; bottom: mugs, "Piggy Blues," "Sprout," "Lyonnaise," "Bunny"

"Cry Baby" cereal, "Yellow Rabbit" plate, "Sprout" mug, Astor shape

"Bunny Hop," Skyline shape

"Duck in Hat" plate and cereal, Skyline shape

"Flower Children" set, Astor shape

"Humpty" set, Skyline shape

"Circus" set, Skyline shape

Three Little Pigs cereal

Three Little Pigs plate, Clinchfield shape

Three Little Pigs mug, shows the Practical Pig

Marks used on Three Little Pigs pieces

Divided bowl and mug from Mickey Mouse set

Feeding dish made for a special little girl

Feeding dish, "Baby's Pets" for a little boy

"Burro" pattern, Skyline shape

Child's tea set, "French Peasant" pattern, Colonial shape

"Painted Daisy"

Fabulous Finds: Artist-signed Pieces

The wonderful artist signed turkey platters, plates, and cups and saucers are the cream of the crop as far as most collectors are concerned. To be considered "artist signed" the signature must be on the front of the piece near the lower right-hand edge. When you find someone's name on the back of a rather ordinary piece, it generally means that the decorator did the item for themselves and wanted to be able to identify it when it came out of the kiln. Artists were allowed to do this to some extent.

The "Wild Turkey" platter (originally called "Turkey Hen") is modeled after Audubon's wild turkey. Our platter has the turkey facing forward, whereas Audubon has her looking back. In *Birds of America* by Audubon, the wild turkey had the place of honor in the very beginning of the volume. The portrait shows the turkey walking through the cane that is characteristic of the riverbanks and swamps of the South. It was probably painted in 1825 while Audubon was in Louisiana. Our Blue Ridge platter was signed by artist Mae Garland and is on the 17½" Clinchfield shape.

"Wild Turkey" Audubon print from baby elephant folio

"Wild Turkey" 17½" Clinchfield platter, signed Mae Garland. Also shown is Indian Head Character Jug.

"Turkey Gobbler," 17½", Clinchfield platter, signed Mae Garland

"Turkey Gobbler" cup & saucer, Colonial shape, signed Mae Garland

The "Turkey Gobbler" platter is also on the 17½" Clinchfield shape and for years we thought he was all there was in this lovely pattern. Then suddenly a dinner plate, cup, and saucer came to light. These are on the Colonial shape. The big Clinchfield platter shown is signed by artist Mae Garland, as are the cup and saucer. The dinner plate is signed by artist Alleene Miller.

152

"Turkey Gobbler" plate, Colonial shape, signed Alleene Miller

Personally, my favorite artist-signed piece is the Quail Plate. This is another pattern taken from Audubon's California quail found in the original water-color paintings by John James Audubon for the *Birds of America* and also in the baby elephant folio of *Birds of America*. His drawing dates from

Quail from Audubon print from baby elephant folio

about 1837 and shows the female quail (at left) reaching for a spider. Southern Potteries artists added the leaf sprays and accented the mountains. This plate is on the 11¾" Colonial shape and is signed by artist Frances Kyker.

About four years ago, the gorgeous Quail platter shown here made itself known. So far it is the only one we have heard of and is on the Skyline shape. There is *no* artist signature, believe it or not!

The very appealing series of old Mill and Cabin plates are favorites of many collectors. The "Gold Cabin" and the "Yellow Cabin" are identical except for background color. They measure 10½" in diameter on the Clinchfield shape. The "Gold Cabin"

"Quail" plate, Colonial shape, signed Frances Kykr

"Quail" platter, Skyline shape, artist unknown

"Gold Cabin," 10½", Clinchfield shape, artist Ruby S. Hart

153

"Yellow Cabin," 10½", Clinchfield shape, artist Ruby S. Hart (L), "Flower Cabin" on 10½" Clinchfield shape, artist Frances Kyker (R)

shown is signed by Nelsene Q. Calhoun. The Yellow Cabin is the work of artist Ruby S. Hart.

The predominantly green Flower Cabin (on the right) is also 10½" in diameter on the Clinchfield shape and is signed by artist Frances Kyker. Frances told us she could do an unbelievable twelve plates in one day!

Bill loves old mills, so the White Mill and Green Mill plates are favorites of his. They are both on the Clinchfield shape and measure 10½" in diameter. White Mill is signed by artist Nelsene Q. Calhoun, while the Green Mill was done by artist Ruby S. Hart.

Now for the gorgeous pieces that are *not* artist signed, but certainly should be! First we have another Audubon-inspired subject, the black duck. Audubon's painting was probably done about 1832 – 1834 on the Atlantic coast. Audubon wanted to be sure to show the white underwing characteristic of

"White Mill," 10½", Clinchfield shape, artist Nelsene Q. Calhoun

"Black Duck," 17½", Clinchfield platter, not signed

"Green Mill," 10½", Clinchfield shape, artist Nelsene Q. Calhoun

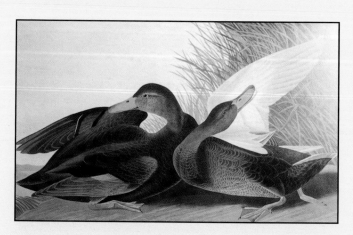

Black Duck Audubon print from Birds of America, 17½", Clinchfield shape, not signed

the species. This lovely platter is on the 13½"
Clinchfield shape.

We understand that Southern Potteries had
planned, but never produced, a much larger line of
Audubon Birds. This colorful 12" platter on the
Colonial shape has the Blue Ridge script mark and
the word "Shoveler" on the back. Again, not artist
signed, but surely worth being signed.

"Winter," 17½", Clinchfield platter, not signed

"Shoveler Duck," 12", Colonial shape, not signed

*"Mountain Fisherman," 17½", Clinchfield platter, by
Lola Johnson Bailey*

"Mallard Pair," 17½", Clinchfield platter, not signed

A recent find is the lovely 17½" "Mallard" platter
on Clinchfield shape. Again, not artist signed, but I
can't imagine why not.

"Winter" platter, using the 17½" Clinchfield
platter shape, is not artist signed, but is a lovely
example of a primitive or folk style landscape's.

In 1941, artist Lola Johnson Bailey did this
huge scenic Fisherman platter as a gift for her husband, who is depicted fishing at his favorite place
in Rocky Fork. The platter is marked only with the
recipient's birth date on the back. This is a great
piece of folk art and needless to say, it is treasured

"Wilson's Retreat," Colonial plate, not signed

by the artist's family. We thank the artist's grand-
daughter, Leslie Bailey for this photo.

This lovely Colonial shape "Wilson's Retreat"
plate turned up at the Erwin, Tennessee, Blue Ridge

show in 1998. We're calling the pattern "Wilson's Retreat" in honor of owner Bonnie Wilson from Kentucky who claims the building looks just like her homeplace. Again, it is *not* artist signed.

The "Driftwood" fish platter was shown on eBay, described as follows: "This platter once belonged to Mr. Hugh Kibler, president of Southern Potteries here in Erwin, Tennessee. It was made to commemorate three fishing buddies and their trip/trips to Driftwood in Vero Beach, Florida. Artist signed under the smaller of the fish by Geo. M (Georgia Miller), artist at Blue Ridge Pottery. Names under the larger fish were the fishing buddies. It is back stamped with the pine tree mark and decorated on the back and initialed by Mr. Kibler himself. Dated 3-1-54."

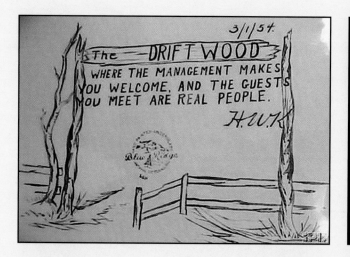

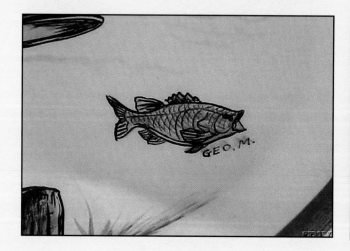

"Driftwood" fish platter, Clinchfield, signed GEO.M.

Character Jugs

A line of china (porcelain) Character Jugs was introduced in the mid-1950s. The line consisted of Paul Revere (6½"), Daniel Boone (6"), the Pioneer Woman (6½"), and the Indian (6¾"). They were expensive for the time and in the end, not many were made. Some have a Blue Ridge mark, usually the round pine tree mark, but by no means all. Some will be found with Daniel Boone, Paul Revere, or Pioneer Woman incised into the underside but again, not all. The Indian was not incised for some unknown reason.

Facial color and background colors were sprayed on; all else was painstakingly hand painted. The Johnson twins who decorated most of the jugs, claim they could do twelve a day!

Pioneer Woman, 6½" tall, full face

Pioneer Woman, profile

Indian Jug, 6¾" tall

Daniel Boone, 6" tall, full face

Daniel Boone, profile, note coonskin tail handle.

For years, all the decorators and other workers told us there was only one size made of the Pioneer Woman. However, what should come to light in recent years, but a little version only about 4" tall, with identical coloring and also incised Pioneer Woman. We have learned that samples were made of the smaller size but it was found that they took every bit as much work as the larger counterpart. Since the little one could not be sold for as much as the larger version, it was found not to be profitable to produce.

Therefore, the samples that were made — how many no one knows — are all that exist.

Sometimes collectors are confused over the Character Jugs made by the Cash Family Pottery (Clinchfield Artware Pottery). Keep in mind that Southern Pottery jugs are made of porcelain while the Cash Family jugs are earthenware. Porcelain, by nature, will shrink more in the mold and thus come out smaller than the earthenware version. Also, Cash pieces are usually marked as such.

The first Southern Pottery products to be copied and unfortunately sold to unsuspecting collectors as the real thing, were Character Jugs. So how does one tell whether the often unmarked jug you're looking at is Southern Potteries or not? The simple way is to look inside the jug where the handle attaches at the top. The handles on Southern Pottery jugs were made separately and attached, making a smooth interior. The reproductions were made with jug and handle all in one piece. This caused a definite hole to appear where the handle formed at the top of the jug, as shown in the following photo. If there is a hole at the top or bottom of the handle, inside the jug, you have a reproduction.

Pioneer Woman, large and small

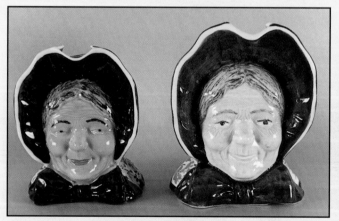

Pioneer Woman, Southern Potteries (L), Cash Family (R)

Paul Revere, copy (L), Daniel Boone, Southern Pottery (R)

China or Porcelain Ware

A line of about 40 pieces of fine quality vitreous (porcelain) chinaware was introduced in about 1945. These items will almost always be marked with the word "china" along with one of the Blue Ridge marks. The exceptions to this rule are the shakers which often did not have room on the base. Some will simply say "china" and some will have no marks at all, but have been found in the original blue printed boxes. Considering the dates of production, this was a fairly expensive line. It was made up of decorative or specialty items such as pitchers, shakers, fancy sugars and creamers, covered boxes, chocolate pots, teapots, vases, fancy relishes, and cake trays. This line also contained the Character Jugs. Some items were made in both the vitreous china and the regular quality earthenware, such as the Betsy Jugs, covered boxes, some teapots, and coffee pots. So, pay attention to your markings.

"Nola," deep shell

"Mayflower Bouquet," deep shell, china

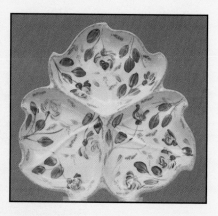

"Rose Parade," Martha snack tray, china. (Martha is the shape name, not the artist.)

"Sweet Violets," deep shell, china

"Rose of Sharon" chocolate tray, china

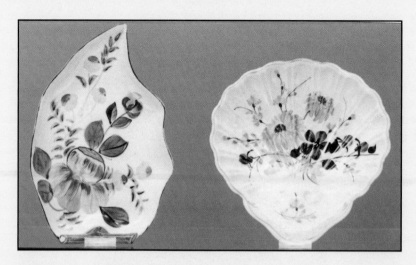

"Rose Garden," Mod Leaf tray, china (L), "Tussie Mussie," deep shell, china (R)

"Serenade" loop handle relish, china (L), "Candied Fruit" heart-shaped relish, china (R)

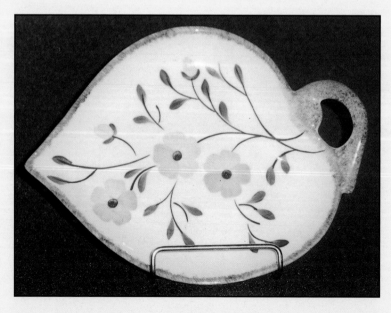

"Anniversary Song" heart relish, china

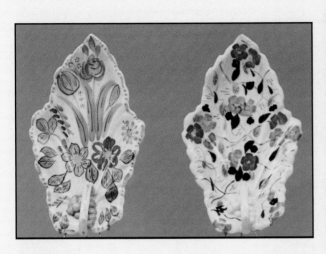

"*Summertime*" *leaf celery, china (L), "Rose of Sharon" leaf celery, china (R)*

"*Fox Grape," leaf celery, china*

"*Butterfly on Leaf" celery, china*

Flat shell bonbons, "Pixie" and "Palace," China. (Palace may be found with "Your gift from the Palace" on the back.)

"Sugar Run" flat shell bonbon, china

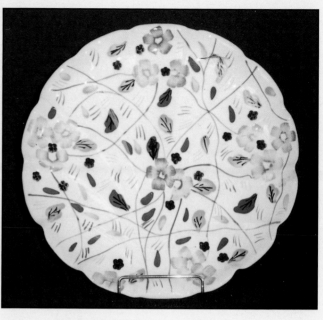

"Rose of Sharon" flat shell bonbon, china

Mark on "Dry Leaf" celery

"Dry Leaf" celery, china

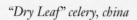

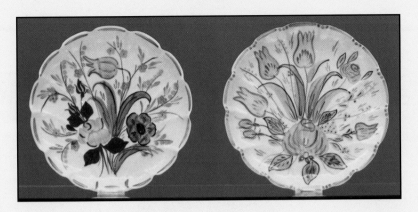

"Evaline" flat shell bonbon (L), "Nove Rose" flat shell bonbon, china (R)

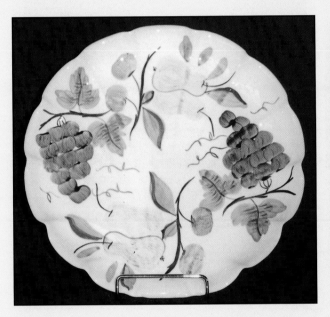

"Orchard" flat shell bonbon, china

"Raining Violets" four-section top handle relish, china

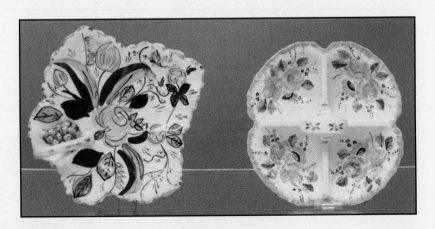

"Verna" Maple Leaf cake tray, china (L), "Ellen" four-section top handle relish, china (R)

Pitchers

"Yellow Peep" Chick

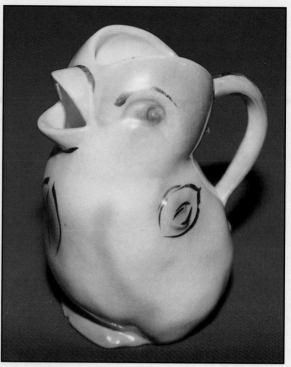

Iridescent Chick

"Polka Dot" Chick

"Ready for my Close-up" fall color
Betsy Jug, china

Line-up of Betsy Jugs, china and earthenware

Palisades, "Red Barn"

"Wild Strawberry," Jane shape

"Red Barn" (L), "Fall Colors" (R), Rebecca shape, china

"Candied Fruit" (L), "Melody" (R), Rebecca shape, china

"Candied Fruit," Sally shape and Rebecca shape

Mini (4½") Virginia shape and Antique (3¼") shape, "Conasauga" pattern, china

Spiral, Jane, and Grace shapes, in "Rose Hill" pattern, china

"Anniversary Song" mini Antique (3¼") pitcher, mini (4½") round vase, 4½" Virginia shape mini pitcher

"Melody," Grace shape

"Fox Grape," Spiral

"Calico," Clara shape

"Fox Grape," Antique shape, china

"Veronica," Antique shape, china

"Fish Tale," Antique shape, china

"Nove Rose," Antique shape, china

"Lyonnaise" Lady, Antique shape

"Lyonnaise" Gentleman, Antique shape

Palisades with pink flower

Grace shape Cobalt Splatter china, plain rose earthenware, "Nove Rose," Clara (5½"), china

Tea, Coffee & Chocolate Pots

Green Briar, Piecrust (L), "Fairmede Fruits," square round (R)

Painted by Lola Johnson Bailey (initials L.J.B. on each piece, even lids)

"Baby Doll" square round teapot

"Darkly" square round teapot

"Spring Song" square round teapot

"Susan," Skyline (L), "Spider Web"
Skyline teapot (R)

"Shepherd's Purse" Skyline teapot

"Tiny Tim" Skyline teapot

"Pink Bluefield" Skyline teapot

"Normandy" Skyline teapot

"Jigsaw" Ball shape teapot, sugar, and creamer

"Peony" Colonial teapot, sugar, and creamer

Polka Dot Colonial teapot, sugar, and creamer

Painted by Lola Johnson Bailey, Ball shape teapot, sugar, and creamer

"Lyonnaise" Ball shape teapot

"Winery" Ball shape teapot

"Wanda's Wild Rose" mini Ball pedestal sugar and creamer, bud top salt and pepper

"Red Barn" weathervane variant snub nose teapot

"Leesa" Good Housekeeping shape teapot

"Tulip" demi pot

"Spring Bouquet" demi set, china

Charm House set, china

"Cock 'o the Morn" Woodcrest teapot

"Grandmother's Garden" ovoid coffee pot

Left to right: "Blackberry Lily," "Wild Strawberry," "Bluebell Bouquet," "Flower Ring" ovoid coffee pots

"Ridge Rose" chocolate set

"Midnight" chocolate set

"Rose Marie" chocolate pot, sugar, and creamer on Elegance tray

"Moonlight" chocolate set, same pattern as above, different trim

"Red Barn" chocolate pot, sugar, and creamer

"Barn and Silo" carafe (L), "Square Dancers" carafe (R)

"Swiss Dancers" chocolate pot

This Is

**GENUINE BLUE RIDGE
HAND-PAINTED UNDERGLAZE
CHINA**

It Is Identified As

CHOCOLATE POT

Slip found inside chocolate pot at store

Lamps, Vases & Boxes

Group of lamp bases, left to right, top: "Indian Summer," "Augusta," "Daisy Mae," "Pink Bow," "Diamond Lil"; bottom: "Gilbertine," "Tafoya Tulip"

Wall sconce cup for base, saucer back plate, nice with flickering candle flame bulb

"Fox Grape" saucer with metal fittings for candle lamp

Group of round vases. Left to right, top: "Anniversary Song," "Nove Rose," "Candied Fruit"; bottom: "Melody," "Rose of Sharon," "Pink Passion Flowers"

Both sides of "Elegance" on ruffle top shape, china

"French Peasant" ruffle top vase

Vase with label "Wrisley's Bath Salts — adds perfume & benefits to the bath."

"Mood Indigo" tapered vase (L), "Gladys" Boot (R), comes in 8½" only

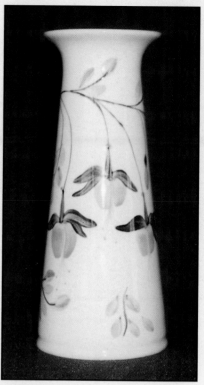

"Purple Crown" tapered vase

Bud vases, hard to find

"Roseworth" candy box

"Sherman Lily" box, "American Beauty" pattern. This gorgeous box can be found embellished with many different patterns.

"Sherman Lily" box, "Dimity" pattern

"Sherman Lily" box, "Melody" pattern

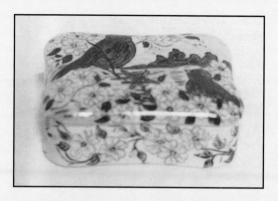

"Sherman Lily" box. The lily was broken off so this bluebird pattern was painted instead. This the only one found to date.

Individual ashtray, "Naughty" pattern (L), square cigarette box, "Sheree," 4½" (R)

"Mallard" box (5½" x 4¾") with "Streamside" pattern, "Streamside" ashtray to match (L), "Whig Rose" ashtrtay (R)

"Sunset Sails" square cigarette box with ashtray, four trays in box

"Heather Bouquet" candy box

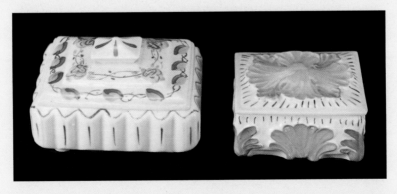

"Rose Step" (4¾" x 5¼") box, china (L), "Seaside" (3½" x 4½"), china (R)

"Dancing Nude" box, 4", very scarce

"Lyonnaise" cigarette box and ashtrays

"Conasauga" square cigarette box with ashtray

Tea Tiles

"Red Apple"

"Crab Apple"

"Victory Garden"

"Sparks Violets," decorated by Kathryn Sparks

"Summer Day"

"Ridge Rose"

"Fragrance" (L), "Carrie" (R)

"Golden Girl"

"Delores"

"Minnesota Rose"

"Rosemae"

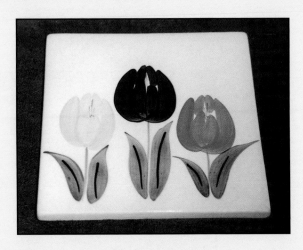

"Spring Peepers"

Poinsettia

"Cowslip"

"Pinkie Lee"

"Bells"

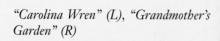
"Carolina Wren" (L), "Grandmother's
Garden" (R)

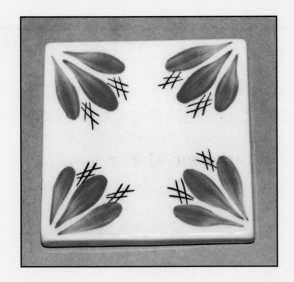

"Quartet"

"Butterfly and Berry"

"Rooster"

"Cherry Fizz"

"French Peasant" tiles, square and round

This "Bicycle Built for Two" tile was decorated by artist Ruby Hart for fellow artist Kathryn Sparks. The girls in vintage clothing are riding full-tilt down the mountain. Red-haired Kathryn is yelling "Look out Ruby" while brave Ruby in the front seat says "Come on Kathryn."

This "Frank Sparks" tile was decorated by Southern's head designer, Lena Watts, as a gift for artist Kathryn Sparks. It shows Kathryn's husband, Frank, on his way to Fort Ogelthorp for his stint in the military. Frank's knees are shaking and tears are falling. Behind the tree is the coach waving and calling By(e) Frank while Frank's faithful dog is howling a mournful wooooo. We are happy to report that Frank did come home from the war healthy and happy.

If you're very good, someday you may end up with a collection like this!

Ashthrays

Evidently, Southern Potteries did a good deal of business in ashtrays, judging from the number of them available. Many carried advertising for various companies or organizations and make a fascinating collection all by themselves. The main shapes are the 5 – 5½" round trays and the "eared" shape. Also found will be the squared individual trays and the rectangular trays that go with the covered cigarette boxes.

"Jodee" advertising tray

Theater Premium Co. advertising tray, note New York address

Bristol Twins baseball team, two different trays shown

ET & WNC Transportation Co. advertising tray

Sometimes the advertising was on the back of the tray.

Pair of advertising trays for Clinchfield Railroad

Ashtray and bread tray commemorating Herbert Hoover's one major campaign speech in the South, held in Elizabethton, Tennessee. The Hoover Banquet was held in Johnson City, Tennessee, following the speech on October 6, 1928. All writing is in gold.

Hoover & Curtis advertising tray

This advertising tray shows the Confederate Monument in Stone Mountain, Georgia.

Advertising tray for Clinchfield Railroad Co.

"Bountiful" ashtray

"Show Off" ashtray

Selection of china trays that fit into the Mallard Box shape

Two of the eared trays. On the back of the right hand tray is Compliments of the People's Bank, Johnson City, TN

Bernice, Unicoi, Tenn. Nov. 6, 1944 (L), Steve, Bill & Alma on back, plus B.G. Nov. 6, 1944 (R). Were these folks going on a cruise together or just daydreaming?

Sponged blue edge, touched with gold, probably early

"Contrary Mary," on back is S.P.I. Inc., Warranted gold 22K, Made in USA all in gold lettering

"Violet" ashtray

"Nove Rose" ashtray, signed on back by Aleene Miller

Selection of 5" round and eared ashtrays

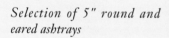

Selection of 5" round and eared ashtrays

Selection of trays sized for Mallard shape box

"Border Print" ashtray

Selection of advertising ashtrays

Kitchenware

In the mid-1950s, a line of ovenware or kitchenware was introduced. Many pieces carried no marks at all or were simply marked "Oven Proof" in the familiar Southern Potteries script. Others used the regular ovenware backstamp illustrated in the chapter on Marks or were marked with a jobber's logo.

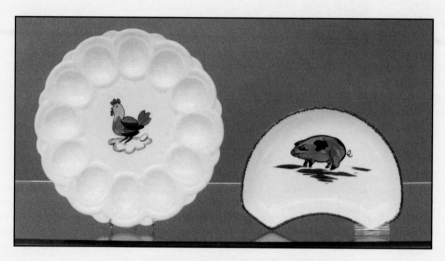

"Rooster" egg plate (L), "Piggie" individual relish (R)

"Twin Tulip" egg plate

Back of Southern Potteries egg plate. Plates made by others have a very similar front, but a different back shape.

Batter set: syrup, 5½" tall; batter jug, 8" tall; tray, 13⅜" long; syrup is hard to find

Three of the "Daisy Chain" mixing bowls, the set of four measured 9x4", 7½x4", 6⅛x3¼", and 6x2⅞"

Three "Leaf" mixing bowls, same sizes as Daisy Chain

"Renegade" heavy pie baker

Egg cups, left to right: "Country Road," "Roseanna," "Weathervane," "Big Apple," "Violets"

Three "Mountain Crab" stacking leftovers

"Butterfly & Leaves" rectangular divided baker

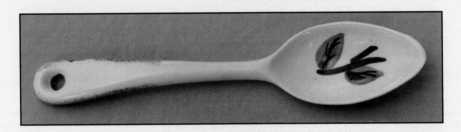

Serving spoon

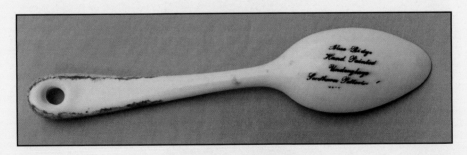

Serving spoon showing backstamp

"Gumdrop Leaf" covered casserole and underplate

"Maynard" small shouldered bowl, early

10" heavy divided plate marked "Mt. Glory, Blue Ridge Mountain Hand Art" on back

Small "French Peasant" covered leftover

"Border Print" set

Two "Kitchenette" covered leftovers

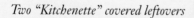

Sets to Collect

❧ ❧

Have you ever noticed that a whole set or collection of one pattern suddenly becomes much more attractive than a single piece — or two — of the same pattern? The following pages will show a number of sets or partial sets in all their colorful glory. We bet they will encourage you to find more pieces in your favorite pattern.

"Orchard" chinaware

"Rose of Sharon"

"Conasauga," mostly china

"Candied Fruit," china

"Calico," china

"Anniversary Song," china

"Melody," china

"Melody," china

"Garden Lane"

"Red Barn," china

"Nove Rose," china

Charm House, china

"Romance"

Good Housekeeping

"Midnight" black border pieces

"Fall Colors"

"Chintz" tea and coffee pots and pitchers

"Swiss Dancers," china

"French Peasant" cake plate and lifter

"French Peasant"

"French Peasant" breakfast set

"French Peasant" demi cups, saucers, sugar, creamer, and tray along with ovoid coffee pot

"Violets"

"Bluebell Bouquet" demi set

Left to right: "Sailboat," Astor; "Windjammer," Clinchfield; "Ship Ahoy," Astor; "Mariner," Candlewick

"Brittany" demi pieces

"Countryside" set, top, left to right: 9" "Pumpkin" plate, 10" "Blackberry Vine" plate, 9" "Shelling Peas" soup bowl, 6" "Breezy Window" plate, "Egg Basket" berry bowl, "Straw Hat" saucer, "Mushrooms" creamer, "Trellis & Flowers" sugar

Matching Glassware

In the mid-1940s a small glass factory was started in Bowling Green, Ohio, by Earl Newton, a Southern Potteries sales representative. His decorators learned techniques and patterns from Southern's decorators and he began to produce glassware decorated to match Southern Potteries patterns. Later, he began purchasing glass blanks in various shapes from Libby Glass and Federal Glass, both in clear and frosted backgrounds.

A Lancaster, Ohio, glass decorating shop known as Gay Fad Studios operated from 1943 to 1963. They also purchased blanks from various large glassmakers and decorated them. It well may be that some of these decorations also matched Southern Potteries patterns.

So far, we have found glassware to match the following patterns:

Blue Bell Bouquet	Chickory
Crab Apple	Cumberland
Dutch Tulip	Evening Flower
Fondeville Flowers	Garden Lane
Greenbriar	Mountain Ivy
Norma	Petal Point
Poppy Duet	Red Rooster
Ridge Daisy	Ridge Harvest
Ridge Ivy	Rose of Sharon
Sun Bouquet	Tic Tac
Tropical	Vibrant
Weathervane	Whirligig

Ridge Daisy set, left to right: Libby sherbet, Libby juice, Libby tumbler, Libby pitcher, unknown tumbler, Federal tumbler with no green rim edge, Federal tumbler with green stripe, Federal juice with green stripe

Greenbriar

This bowl matches Poinsettia but is it a painted-to-match pattern

Glass on frosted background, left to right: "Sunfire," "Strawberry Sundae," Fruit Fantasy

Assorted frosted glasses, left to right: Strawberry Sundae, Tic-Tac, Sunfire, Poinsettia, Fruit Fantasy, Bluebell Bouquet, Tic-Tac

The Many Facets of Blue Ridge Collecting

Collectors love "doing something" with their collection. Something more than just displaying the pieces in a cabinet or on the wall. We love the following ideas gleaned from collectors everywhere.

One collector had a Provincial Line pattern added to the tilework in her kitchen.

Some folks like to add original shipping boxes to their collection as in this Nocturne pattern done for American Beauty Hand Painted Dinnerware from P.T.P Company. Note that the box doesn't mention Southern Potteries at all!

AMERICAN BEAUTY HAND-PAINTED
DINNERWARE
UNIT NO. 1
1 DINNER PLATE
1 CUP
1 SAUCER
P.T.P. CO., 352 W 44TH ST., NEW YORK 36, N.Y.

Box for above "Nocturne" set

This collector had a special 43" wrought iron rack made to hold her cake lifter collection. The rack, which included a stylized version of the round Pine Tree mark was designed by Doug Shank.

These lovely hand-painted Christmas ornaments are signed "Suzanne '96"

A motif from an embroidered luncheon cloth, suggesting Daisy Chain dinnerware

Not having any luck with your flower garden? Season over? Try planting a few injured Blue Ridge plates to brighten things up.

An unusual piece to collect is this "French Peasant" plate with ribbon trim evidently sandwiched between the original plate and a cardboard backing. The backing is stamped "Ribbon Trimmed Decorated Wall Plate by Owen." The cardboard backing even has "chips," you will notice.

Cardboard plate backing

A plateful of great hand-decorated cookies made by a collector for their local Blue Ridge Club meeting in Minnesota.

Another plateful of those cookies! Yuummmm!

This photo was taken of a 1950 model kitchen at Pioneer Village, Menden, Nebraska. The popular chrome table is set with Quaker Apple

A mouth-watering section of one of the booths at the annual Blue Ridge Show in Erwin, Tennessee.

Old Clinchfield Ware

Until recently, the bulk of the old Clinchfield Ware produced from about 1917 until the mid-1930s, did not particularly interest collectors. Decoration was decal, gold lining, and trim very much like the product of hundreds of other potteries of the era. However, there are facets of the production that make nice additions to the Southern Potteries collection, such as the often-found wide, richly colored plate borders covered with gold lace. The elaborate and quite interesting Brotherhood of Operative Potters mark found on some pieces appeals to Southern Potteries collectors. The bowls, plates, and pitchers that carry advertising or special order messages such as Christmas greetings are fun to collect. The plates were originally advertised as "Souvenir Plaques."

Also of interest are the luster-decorated fish sets, consisting of a platter with smaller matching plates. The Crusader Series of plates made with the logo "Van Dyne" are a great addition to a collection of old Clinchfield Ware, as are items depicting historical places or carrying portraits of famous people. Occasionally, one will find a platter or plate decorated with a transfer or decal of a K. T. Beck painting. These usually feature cows or other animals. Mr. Beck designed scenes for many different companies. The signature on the piece is part of the transfer, not an artist signature.

Collectors should keep in mind that the marks used by the Cash Family Pottery include the words "Clinchfield Art Ware." If the words "art" or "Cash Family" appear in the mark, the product is *not* from Southern Potteries.

Creamer, covered sugar, and handled cup in white luster with fold trim, inside edge of cup has pale orange luster band

Gold Braid pattern milk pitcher

10½" luster edge bowl with flowers (L), 11½" luster rolled-edge bowl (R)

Commemorative plates, left to right: Robert E. Lee 9" plate, Robert E. Lee 8" square plate, 9" Stone Mountain Memorial plate

Large fish platter with luster, main piece in a Fish set

9½" plate for Fish set (L), 9¼" "Bluebirds & Blossoms" plate (R)

"Bluebirds & Blossoms" cup and saucer

"Eden" bowl with crown mark

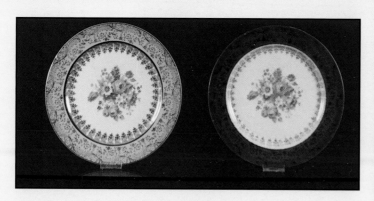

Two 10½" plates with the gold lace overlay on wide borders, plate with wine-colored border says "Compliments of Frank T. Gentry, Superintendent of Schools, Unicoi County, Dec. 1941."

"Cows in Pasture" platter with orange luster border, K.T. Back painting, done on a transfer or decal

Following are the Crusader Series plates. All have crown mark along with "Van Dyne" in gold lettering.

March Through the Desert

The Defender of the Cross

Converted to the Christian Faith

The Arrival Before Jerusalem

Offering a Prayer After the Battle

A Dangerous Intruder

This Roman Couple carries the same Van Dyne mark, but probably was not included in the Crusader Series. Plate has a helmeted head at the top of the front.

Advertising plates, legend says: "O.E.S. Birmingham, Alabama, Grand Chapter of Alabama, Oct. 17, 18, 19, 1927, reverse side "Betsy Ross Bread, McGough Bakeries Corp., Birmingham, Ala." (L), Candlewick, "Christmas Greetings from Campbell's Service Station, Hampton, Tennessee" (R)

Lotus Leaf, "Red Willow," probably 1930s

George Washington plate, marked "P.T.A. Erwin, Tennessee"

Lotus Leaf advertising bowl

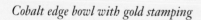

Legend on above bowl

Cobalt edge bowl with gold stamping

Watauga bowl "Fabulous" pattern, "Compliments of Ritter Furniture Company, Nashville, Tenn."

Teapot with "Rose Scroll" pattern

Covered vegetable bowls, top: "Bluebirds & Blossoms," bottom: "Lone Bluebird"

"Solitary Rose" bowl on Wautauga shape

"Yellow Tea Rose" 10½" bowl with crown mark

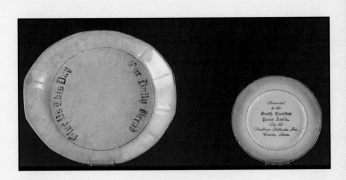

Give Us This Day Our Daily Bread platter, on reverse is "Compliments of Pouder Furniture Co, Elizabeth, Tenn., opposite court house" in gold (L), 7" plate Presented to the South Carolina Press Association by the Southern Potteries Inc., Erwin, Tenn. (R)

"Black Beauty" decal and gold on Candlewick shape

"Santa Maria" bowl

8" Lace Edge fish plate, logo reads: "Compliments of T.A. Watson, Medville, Kansas"

"Steamer" bowl

Confederate Monument plate, Stone Mountain, Georgia. Shown are Robert E. Lee, Stonewall Jackson and Jefferson Davis on horseback. There are troops in the background that do not appear on the actual monument.

Marks

Old Clinchfield Marks

CLINCHFIELD
S. P. I

Southern Pottery Marks

Southern Potteries, Inc.
Warranted Gold 22 Kt.
Made in U. S. A.

Southern
Potteries, Inc.
WARRANTED
22 KT. GOLD
DECORATED
MADE IN U. S. A.

Underglaze
Hand-Painted
S. P. Inc.
Erwin, Tenn.
Oven Proof

Underglaze
Hand Painted
Southern Potteries, Inc.
MADE IN U. S. A.

This Is

GENUINE BLUE RIDGE
HAND-PAINTED UNDERGLAZE
CHINA

It Is Identified As

CHOCOLATE POT

Underglaze
Hand Painted
Southern Potteries
BAKE
WARE
MADE IN
U.S.A.

Underglaze
Hand Painted
J. P. Inc.
Erwin, Tenn.
Oven Proof

Blue Ridge
Hand Painted
Underglaze
MADE IN U.S.A.

Underglaze
Hand Painted
Made Especially for
Blair

SOUTHERN
POTTERIES, INC.
ERWIN, TENN.

This mark found on animal figures.

Reproductions

"*Countryside*"
HAND PAINTED
UNDERGLAZE
SOUTHERN POTTERIES, INC.
MADE IN U.S.A.

Although Southern did make some things for Fondeville, this mark is found on items that are not Southern Potteries.

Reproduction not Southern Potteries

This mark is often found on restaurant ware and is not Southern Potteries.

The Jobber Jumble

There has been some confusion regarding the various jobber marks used on Southern Potteries products, especially in the case of the PV in a circle. First of all, keep in mind that a jobber or wholesaler buys merchandise for resale from many different manufacturers, sometimes having the jobber's own mark applied to the product, and sometimes not.

The PV mark stands for "Peasant Village" which was a trademark used by Mittledorfer Straus, Inc. of New York City. Southern Potteries did many items for Peasant Village, but so did other potteries. Just because an item is marked PV does not mean it is a Southern Potteries product. You have to pay strict attention to whether the item is on a Southern blank or shape; whether it is hand painted under the glaze; whether, indeed, it "looks Southern."

The French Opera plate series marked PV that turns up here and there is a good example of how confusing reproductions and marks can be. As I understand it, the original series of plates were late nineteenth century European products. Around the time of World War II when imports were cut off, Mittledorfer Straus had the plates made in this country and marked with the PV symbol. The same plates were also made by Vernon Kilns in California and scribed with *their* marks and an explanation that they were reproductions.

Another jobber mark that is often seen on Southern Potteries products and also on Japanese ware is the UCAGO (United China and Glass Company) logo. In fact, I understand this is the company that at one point took Blue Ridge to Japan and had it reproduced. Check your UCAGO mark and be sure it is "Made in U.S.A." and not Japan.

A mark we have sometimes found on boots is the Ebeling and Rauss Company of Devon and later Royersford, Pennsylvania. This mark will often be found with a drawing of a bell incorporated into it. Ebeling and Rauss went bankrupt in the mid-1980s, I understand, and all records were disposed of. They are now back in business in Allentown, Pennsylvania, having been purchased by Ronald Rapelje in 1992. They are strictly a wholesaler for the gift shop trade; they do not make any pottery themselves.

The Stanhome Ivy pattern has confused a lot of folks because you can find three different marks on the same pattern and shape. There is the special Stanhome mark, the Blue Ridge mark, and the Cannonsburg mark. This was a puzzler, but we have discovered the reason for the Cannonsburg mark. It seems that after Southern Potteries closed, a group of the decorators moved to the Cannonsburg Pottery and for over a year, painted the Stanhome Ivy pattern and others for Cannonsburg. Thus the three different marks. Only the Stanhome mark or the Blue Ridge mark is actually a Southern Potteries product. See the Marks Section in this book for other jobbers that bought from Southern Potteries.

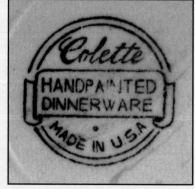

Cumberland
Hand Painted
Dinnerware
MADE IN U.S.A.

TULIP
Underglaze
Hand Painted
MADE IN U.S.A.

P L
C
COLONIAL
FARNIE
U.S.A.
Hand Painted
Underglaze

Prim Rose China
NATIONAL BROTHERHOOD
CO-OPERATIVE POTTERS
HAND PAINTED
UNDER GLAZE

RICHMOND
SOUTHERN HAND PAINTED
MADE
ERWIN, TENN.
U.S.A.
CLINCHFIELD WARE

MOUNTAIN CRAB
BLUE RIDGE MOUNTAINS
HAND ART

VITAMIN FROLICS
CLINCHFIELD
BLUE RIDGE MOUNTAINS
HAND ART

Underglaze
Hand Painted
MADE IN
U. S. A.
LAUREL WREATH

VALLEY BLOSSOM
BLUE RIDGE MOUNTAINS
HAND ART

OVENPROOF
PRIMROSE

SUN CHINA CO.
MADE IN U.S.A.
WARRANTED
22 KT. GOLD

Rosebuds
HANDPAINTED
DINNERWARE
MADE IN U.S.A.

"Royal"
OVEN WARE
GUARANTEED 100%
OVEN PROOF
MADE IN
U. S. A.

P.V.

Good Housekeeping
Genuine China

RED LEAF
HAND PAINTED
UNDERGLAZE
MADE IN U. S. A.

R. H E. Co.
2244-U
UNION MADE
IN U.S.A.

KING'S
HAND PAINTED
UNDERGLAZE
MADE IN U.S.A.

WESTWOOD
Underglaze
Hand Painted
MADE IN U. S. A.

FONDEVILLE
NEW YORK

Vicago
Underglaze
Hand Painted
U.S.A.

Charm House
FIVE
CHINA
C G
HAND
PAINTED

NASCO
Underglaze
Hand Painted
MADE IN
U. S. A.

Sunshine
Hand Painted
Dinnerware
MADE IN U.S.A.

BERKSHIRE
Underglaze
Hand Painted
MADE IN U. S. A.

BEVERLEY
Underglaze
Hand Painted
MADE IN U. S. A.

NASCO
22 KT. DEC
EMPRESS
MADE IN U.S.A.

Mount Vernon
Hand Painted
UNDERGLAZE
MADE IN U.S.A.

BLUE WILLOW
UNDERGLAZE
A FRANKLIN KENT
CREATION
MADE IN U. S. A.

American Home
Genuine China

WESTFALL
CHINA CO.
HAND PAINTED

PROVINCIAL
BLUE RIDGE MOUNTAINS
HAND ART

PRICE THEATRE PREMIUMS CO.
TELEPHONE
CIRCLE 6-1298
352 W. 44th ST.
NEW YORK 18, N. Y.

WILSHIRE
Underglaze
Hand Painted
MADE IN U. S. A.

Advertisements

If you choose this spriggy wallpaper, "Blossom Tree," there is china to match in color and design. A single tree, straight from the wallpaper, is the motif. In all five of these china-wallpaper combinations, one chinaware color blends with various wallpaper grounds.

Now your china

can match your walls

Are you a stickler for perfectionist matching?

See how made-for-each-other combinations of

wallpaper and china can give the finished, luxury l

of "custom" design to a dining area or kitchen

DINNERSET COMPOSITION

Comp. "A"
16 pcs. — List $1.27
4 Cups
4 Saucers
4 Plates 7"
4 Fruits 4"

Comp. "B"
20 pcs. — List $1.54
Same as Comp. "A"
plus 4 Plates 4"

Comp. "C"
22 pcs. — List $1.91
Same as Comp. "A"
plus 4 Plates 4"
1 Nappy 7"
1 Platter 8"

Comp. "D"
32 pcs. — List $2.67
6 Cups
6 Saucers
6 Plates 7"
6 Plates 4"
6 Fruits 4"
1 Nappy 7"
1 Platter 8"

Comp. "E"
35 pcs. — List $3.27
Same as Comp. "D"
plus 1 Cream
1 Cvd. Sugar

Comp. "F"
41 pcs. — List $3.92
Same as Comp. "D"
plus 6 Coupes 6"
1 Cream
1 Cvd. Sugar

Comp. "G"
42 pc. — List $4.06
Same as Comp. "D"
plus 6 Coupes 6"
1 Cream
1 Cvd. Sugar
1 Plate 8"

Comp. "H"
45 pcs. — List $4.17
8 Cups
8 Saucers
8 Plates 7"
8 Plates 4"
8 Fruits 4"
1 Nappy 7"
1 Platter 10"
1 Cvd. .Sugar
1 Cream

Comp. "I"
50 pcs. — List $4.43
8 Cups
8 Saucers
8 Plates 7"
8 Plates 4"
8 Fruits 4"
8 Coupes 6"
1 Nappy 7"
1 Platter 10"

Comp. "J"
50 pcs. — List $4.70
Same as Comp. "I"
using 8" and 5" Plates
instead of 7" & 4" Plates

Comp. "K"
53 pcs. — List $5.03
8 Cups
8 Saucers
8 Plates 7"
8 Plates 4"
8 Fruits 4"
8 Coupes 6"
1 Nappy 7"
1 Platter 10"
1 Cvd. Sugar
1 Cream

Comp. "KX"
53 pcs. — List $5.23
Same as Comp. "K"
using 8" Plates instead
of 7" Plates

Comp. "L"
53 pcs. — List $5.30
Same as Comp. "K" using
8" Plates and 5" Plates
instead of 7" Plates and
4" Plates

Comp. "M"
62 pcs. — List $6.17
Same as Comp. "KX"
plus 8 Plates 6"
1 7" Baker

Comp. "N"
93 pcs. — List $9.34
12 Cups
12 Saucers
12 Plates 8"
12 Plates 6"
12 Plates 4"
12 Fruits 4"
12 Coupes 6"
1 Nappy 7"
1 Covered Dish, Rd.
1 Platter 8"
1 Cvd. Sugar
1 Cream
1 Platter 10"
1 Sauce Boat

In any composition the 7" Baker may be substituted for 7" Nappy or Lug Soups for Coupe Soups at no additional cost.

243

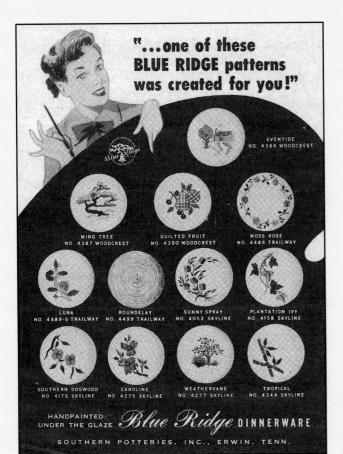

Beauty WITHIN EVERYBODY'S REACH

AUTUMN APPLE
No. 3735 Colonial

BLUE
RIDGE
Dinnerware

SOUTHERN
POTTERIES, INC.

The popular Autumn Apple (No. 3735) on the Colonial shape, symbolizing the bounty of Nature, proclaims generous hospitality at your own table. This delightful Blue Ridge pattern is a luxury well within the reach of all. Priced no higher than ordinary dinnerware, Blue Ridge offers the charm and distinction of Hand Painted patterns with the enduring loveliness of Under the Glaze decorations. There are many other fascinating and practical Blue Ridge creations to delight you, your family and your guests. See them at your dealer's today.

Luxury with Economy!

The big, red, smiling petals of the Blue Ridge Poinsettia Pattern (No. 3545) on the popular Colonial shape will brighten your table and make every meal festive. This pattern brings joy to the homemaker because it radiates the luxuriousness of costly dinnerware at a price within a modest budget. The Poinsettia Pattern is not only brilliant and exquisite but its Hand Painted design Under the Glaze will stay fresh and rich through years of service. For your next gift occasion treat yourself to a gorgeous set of Blue Ridge Ware or make another homemaker happy with Poinsettia or one of the many other lovely patterns at your dealer's.

POINSETTIA
No. 3545 Colonial

BLUE
RIDGE
Dinnerware

SOUTHERN POTTERIES, INC.

Price Guide

Do we really need to mention that this listing of prices should be considered a guide, not a Bible? We see unbelievable prices advertised here and there and in shops and malls but remember the old saying "Askin' ain't gettin'." We try to gather "sold at" prices from various parts of the country and then average them in order to get a good idea of actual sales prices.

Prices listed are for items in perfect condition; no cracks, chips, browning, or large amounts of crazing. We list a range in prices, with the simple patterns at the low end and the more elaborate patterns at the top. China (porcelain) and earthenware prices are listed separately for pieces that were made both ways. Some bodies and lids are also listed separately.

Premium patterns include those with people, barns, houses, roosters, chickens, animals, birds, home interiors, holiday motifs, Mexican and Oriental motifs, pixies, wallpaper patterns, and designer plates, which are fanciful and outrageous but were never placed on the market.

Ashtrays, individual	$18.00 – 20.00
Ashtrays, advertising, railroad	$55.00 – 65.00
Ashtrays, advertising, round	$60.00 – 70.00
Ashtrays with rest (eared)	$20.00 – 30.00
Ashtray, Mallard Box shape	$55.00 – 65.00
Basket, 10" aluminum edge	$30.00 – 35.00
Basket, 7" aluminum edge	$25.00 – 30.00
Bonbon, Charm House, china	$175.00 – 225.00
Bonbon, div. ctr. hdl, china	$85.00 – 100.00
Bonbon, flat shell, china	$55.00 – 75.00
Bonbon, flat shell, Pixie, china	$100.00 – 150.00
Bowl, 5¼" fruit	$7.00 – 10.00
Bowl, 6" cereal/soup	$18.00 – 25.00
Bowl, 6" cereal/soup, Premium	$25.00 – 30.00
Bowl, flat soup	$20.00 – 25.00
Bowl, flat soup, Premium	$25.00 – 35.00
Bowl, hot cereal	$20.00 – 25.00
Bowl, 10½" – 11½" salad	$60.00 – 75.00
Bowl, 11½" Square Dancers	$150.00 – 200.00
Bowl, cov. vegetable	$50.00 – 85.00
Bowl, cov. veg., Premium	$125.00 – 175.00
Bowl, mixing, small	$15.00 – 20.00
Bowl, mixing, medium	$20.00 – 25.00
Bowl, mixing, large	$25.00 – 30.00
Bowl, 8" round veg.	$20.00 – 30.00
Bowl, 9" oval veg.	$25.00 – 35.00
Bowl, 9" round veg. divided	$35.00 – 40.00
Box, 6" rd. cov. candy, china	$125.00 – 150.00
Box, Sq. cigarette only	$85.00 – 90.00
Box, Dancing Nudes, china	$600.00 – 750.00
Box, Mallard Duck	$650.00 – 700.00
Box, round cov. powder	$100.00 – 150.00
Box, Rose Step, china	$110.00 – 150.00
Box, Rose Step, pearlized	$85.00 – 100.00
Box, Seaside, china	$125.00 – 150.00
Box, Seaside w/ashtrays	$200.00 – 250.00
Box, Sherman Lily	$700.00 – 900.00
Breakfast set	$350.00 – 500.00
Breakfast set, Premium	$550.00 – 700.00
Butterdish	$35.00 – 45.00
Butterdish, Woodcrest	$45.00 – 55.00
Butterpat/coaster	$25.00 – 35.00
Cake lifter	$30.00 – 35.00
Cake tray, Maple Leaf, china	$50.00 – 75.00
Carafe, w/lid	$100.00 – 150.00
Casserole, w/lid	$45.00 – 50.00
Celery, Leaf shape, china	$40.00 – 50.00
Celery, Skyline	$30.00 – 40.00
Child's cereal bowl	$125.00 – 160.00
Child's mug	$150.00 – 175.00
Child's plate	$125.00 – 175.00
Child's feeding dish, div.	$175.00 – 200.00
Child's Play Tea Set	$375.00 – 400.00
Chocolate pot	$150.00 – 225.00
Chocolate tray	$450.00 – 500.00
Coffee pot, ovoid shape	$150.00 – 175.00
Counter sign	$500.00 – 575.00
Creamer, regular shapes	$12.00 – 18.00
Creamer, Charm House	$70.00 – 85.00
Creamer, pedestal, china	$50.00 – 65.00

Creamer, demi, china ....$80.00 – 95.00

Creamer, demi, earthenware ....$45.00 – 50.00

Creamer, Fifties shape ....$15.00 – 20.00

Creamer, rope handle ....$12.00 – 15.00

Creamer, sm. Colonial, open ....$15.00 – 20.00

Creamer, lg. Colonial, open ....$18.00 – 25.00

Creamer, Waffle shape ....$12.00 – 15.00

Cup & saucer, demi, china ....$75.00 – 85.00

Cup & saucer, demi, Premium............$100.00 – 150.00

Cup & saucer, Jumbo ....$75.00 – 100.00

Cup & saucer, regular shapes.................$15.00 – 20.00

Cup & saucer, Premium...........................$40.00 – 65.00

Cup & saucer, demi, earthenware ....$25.00 – 30.00

Cup & saucer, Holiday.............................$50.00 – 75.00

Cup & saucer, Turkey & Acorn ....$75.00 – 100.00

Cup & saucer, artist-signed..................$400.00 – 425.00

Custard cup...$18.00 – 22.00

Demi pot, china.....................................$250.00 – 300.00

Demi pot, earthenware..........................$125.00 – 175.00

Dish, 8 x 13" baking, divided ....$25.00 – 30.00

Dish, 8 x 13" baking, plain ....$20.00 – 25.00

Dish, 8 x 13" baking w/metal stand ....$30.00 – 35.00

Egg cup, double.......................................$25.00 – 35.00

Egg cup, Premium....................................$50.00 – 60.00

Egg dish, deviled ....$60.00 – 75.00

Glass, tumbler..$15.00 – 20.00

Glass, dessert cup ....$10.00 – 14.00

Glass, juice tumbler.................................$12.00 – 15.00

Gravy boat ....$25.00 – 35.00

Gravy boat, Premium...............................$35.00 – 55.00

Gravy tray ....$50.00 – 70.00

Jug, character, Pioneer Woman ....$400.00 – 500.00

Jug, character, Daniel Boone.................$400.00 – 500.00

Jug, character, Indian............................$600.00 – 700.00

Jug, character, Paul Revere ....$600.00 – 700.00

Jug, batter w/lid.......................................$65.00 – 75.00

Jug, syrup w/lid.......................................$85.00 – 95.00

Lamp, china ....$125.00 – 150.00

Lamp from pitcher, teapot, etc. ....$70.00 – 80.00

Lazy Susan complete ....$550.00 – 650.00

Lazy Susan, center bowl w/lid ....$175.00 – 225.00

Lazy Susan, side pieces ....$60.00 – 75.00

Lazy Susan, wooden base ....$50.00 – 60.00

Leftover, sm. w/lid...................................$35.00 – 45.00

Leftover, med. w/lid ....$50.00 – 65.00

Leftover, lg. w/lid ....$65.00 – 75.00

Marmite w/lid, Charm House..............$170.00 – 200.00

Pie baker ....$35.00 – 45.00

Pitcher, Abby, china.............................$175.00 – 200.00

Pitcher, Abby, earthenware ....$50.00 – 75.00

Pitcher, Alice, 6¼" earthenware............$150.00 – 200.00

Pitcher, Alice 6", china ....$175.00 – 225.00

Pitcher, Antique, 5", china ....$85.00 – 100.00

Pitcher, Antique, 3½"...........................$150.00 – 175.00

Pitcher, Betsy, china ....$200.00 – 250.00

Pitcher, Betsy, earthenware ....$100.00 – 175.00

Pitcher, Betsy, gold decorated ....$250.00 – 300.00

Pitcher, Charm House...........................$250.00 – 275.00

Pitcher, Chick, china ....$100.00 – 125.00

Pitcher, Clara, china ....$95.00 – 125.00

Pitcher, Grace, china ....$95.00 – 120.00

Pitcher, Helen, china ....$85.00 - 125.00

Pitcher, Jane, china...............................$100.00 – 125.00

Pitcher, Martha, earthenware..................$70.00 – 75.00

Pitcher, Milady, china...........................$125.00 – 185.00

Pitcher, Rebecca ....$175.00 – 225.00

Pitcher, Sally, china ....$185.00 – 250.00

Pitcher, Sculptured Fruit, china..............$75.00 – 95.00

Pitcher, Sculptured Fruit, Petite ....$85.00 – 90.00

Pitcher, 7" Spiral, earthenware ....$45.00 – 55.00

Pitcher, 7" Spiral, china..........................$75.00 – 100.00

Pitcher, 7" Spiral, Premium ....$150.00 – 175.00

Pitcher, 4¼" Spiral, china.....................$180.00 – 220.00

Pitcher, 6½" Virginia, china ....$125.00 – 150.00

Pitcher, 4¼" Virginia, china ....$175.00 – 200.00

Pitcher, Watauga ....$350.00 – 400.00

Plate, advertising, lg. ....$300.00 – 325.00

Plate, artist-signed, 10" ....$325.00 – 450.00

Plate, artist-signed, Gold Cabin ....$350.00 – 450.00

Plate, artist-signed, Quail....................$400.00 – 425.00

Plate, artist-signed, Turkey Gobbler ....$750.00 – 800.00

Plate, 12", aluminum edge ....$40.00 – 45.00

Plate, 14", Square Dance......................$350.00 – 400.00

Plate, 11½" – 12"......................................$50.00 – 65.00

Plate, 11½" – 12", Premium ....$100.00 – 125.00

Plate, 10½" dinner.................$20.00 – 25.00

Plate, 10½" dinner, Premium.................$25.00 – 45.00

Plate, 9¼" dinner.................$18.00 – 22.00

Plate, 9¼" dinner, Premium.................$30.00 – 40.00

Plate, heavy divided.................$40.00 – 50.00

Plate, party w/cup well & cup.................$35.00 – 40.00

Plate, party w/cup well & cup, Premium..$50.00 – 75.00

Plate 8" sq.................$20.00 – 25.00

Plate, 8" Square Dancers (square or round) ..$85.00 – 95.00

Plate, 7" round.................$12.00 – 15.00

Plate, 7" square.................$12.00 – 15.00

Plate 6" round.................$8.00 – 10.00

Plate, 6" square (novelty patterns) ....$70.00 – 85.00

Plate, 6" square, Provincial Farm scenes ..$65.00 – 85.00

Plate, 8½" Bird salad.................$65.00 – 80.00

Plate, 8½" Flower or fruit salad.................$25.00 – 30.00

Plate, 8½" Still Life.................$25.00 – 30.00

Plate, 8½" Language of Flowers.................$80.00 – 90.00

Plate, 11" Specialty.................$150.00 – 200.00

Plate, Designer.................$100.00 – 140.00

Plate, Christmas Tree.................$75.00 – 85.00

Plate, Christmas Doorway.................$85.00 – 95.00

Plate, Thanksgiving Turkey.................$75.00 – 90.00

Plate, Turkey w/acorns.................$95.00 – 125.00

Platter, artist-signed, 15".................$1,200.00 – 1,500.00

Platter, Turkey patterns.................$250.00 – 300.00

Platter, 15" regular patterns.................$50.00 – 55.00

Platters, 12½", 13".................$25.00 – 30.00

Platters, Premium.................add 25 – 30%

Ramekin, 5" w/lid.................$30.00 – 35.00

Ramekin, 7½" w/lid.................$40.00 – 45.00

Relish, Charm House, china.................$175.00 – 200.00

Relish, deep shell, china.................$50.00 – 75.00

Relish, heart shape.................$90.00 – 125.00

Relish, individual, Crescent shape.................$35.00 – 50.00

Relish, Loop Handle, china.................$65.00 – 75.00

Relish, Palisades.................$40.00 – 50.00

Relish, Mod Leaf, china.................$75.00 – 90.00

Relish, T-handle.................$65.00 – 75.00

Salad Fork, china.................$45.00 – 50.00

Salad Spoon, china.................$45.00 – 50.00

Salad Fork, Earthenware.................$50.00 – 60.00

Sconce, wall.................$70.00 – 75.00

Server, wood or metal ctr. handle.................$35.00 – 45.00

Shakers, 1¾" Apple, pair.................$40.00 – 45.00

Shakers, 2¼" Apple, pair.................$55.00 – 60.00

Shakers, 1¾" Apple w/floral, pair.................$45.00 – 50.00

Shakers, Blossom Top, pair.................$75.00 – 85.00

Shakers, Bud Top, pair.................$75.00 – 85.00

Shakers, Charm House, pair.................$150.00 – 175.00

Shakers, Chickens, pair.................$150.00 – 175.00

Shakers, Good Housekeeping, pair.................$125.00 – 150.00

Shakers, Range, pair.................$40.00 – 45.00

Shakers, Mallards, pair.................$400.00 – 450.00

Shakers, Palisades, pair.................$35.00 – 45.00

Shakers, tall footed, china, pair.................$75.00 – 100.00

Shakers, Skyline, pair.................$35.00 – 40.00

Sherbet.................$35.00 – 40.00

Sugar, Charm House.................$95.00 – 110.00

Sugar, Colonial, eared, open.................$18.00 – 25.00

Sugar, Colonial, small, open.................$15.00 – 20.00

Sugar, Pedestal, china.................$50.00 – 65.00

Sugar, regular shapes w/lid.................$18.00 – 25.00

Sugar, Rope Handle, w/lid.................$15.00 – 18.00

Sugar, Square Round, w/lid.................$15.00 – 20.00

Sugar, Waffle, w/lid.................$15.00 – 20.00

Sugar, Woodcrest, w/lid.................$25.00 – 30.00

Tea Tile, 6" round or square.................$75.00 – 95.00

Tea Tile, 3" round or square.................$85.00 – 100.00

Teapot, Ball shape.................$150.00 – 200.00

Teapot, Ball shape, Premium.................$200.00 – 250.00

Teapot, Charm House.................$300.00 – 350.00

Teapot, Chevron handle.................$150.00 – 195.00

Teapot, Colonial.................$95.00 – 150.00

Teapot, Fine Panel, china.................$175.00 – 225.00

Teapot, Good Housekeeping, china.................$175.00 – 225.00

Teapot, Mini Ball, china.................$200.00 – 250.00

Teapot, Palisades.................$125.00 – 150.00

Teapot, Piecrust.................$150.00 – 200.00

Teapot, Rope Handle.................$125.00 – 130.00

Teapot, Skyline.................$110.00 – 125.00

Teapot, Snub Nose, china.................$200.00 – 250.00

Teapot, square round, 7".................$95.00 – 150.00

Teapot, square round, 6" ....$80.00 – 95.00

Teapot, Woodcrest ....$175.00 – 200.00

Tidbit, 2-tier...$30.00 – 40.00

Tidbit, 3-tier...$45.00 – 55.00

Toast, covered ....$125.00 – 175.00

Toast, covered, Premium......................$220.00 – 250.00

Toast, covered, French Peasant............$250.00 – 300.00

Toast, lid only, Premium & Peasant......$200.00 – 250.00

Toast, lid only, regular ....$75.00 – 100.00

Tray, demi, Colonial, 5½" x 7"..............$150.00 – 175.00

Tray, demi, Colonial, French Peasant...$210.00 – 225.00

Tray, demi, Skyline 9½" x 7⅞"...............$100.00 – 150.00

Tray, snack, Martha ....$150.00 – 175.00

Tray, waffle set, 9½" x 13½"...................$100.00 – 125.00

Vase, bud..$225.00 – 250.00

Vase, tapered, china ....$125.00 – 145.00

Vase, handled, china ....$95.00 – 100.00

Vase, 8" boot...$80.00 – 95.00

Vase, 9½" ruffle top, china ....$95.00 – 125.00

Prices for Transfer, Decal, and Luster Decorated Clinchfield

Bowl, Pearlized or Lustre finished............$30.00 – 35.00

Gravy, transfer decorated ....$20.00 – 25.00

Plate, O.E.S. Commemorative.................$65.00 – 75.00

Plate, transfer decorated...........................$20.00 – 25.00

Plate, transfer center, wide gold trim border..$25.00 – 30.00

Plate, Robert E. Lee ....$150.00 – 175.00

Plate, Robert E. Lee, faded transfer $85.00

Platter, "Daily Bread"...............................$50.00 – 75.00

Shakers, decal, Blue Willow type, pair......$45.00 – 50.00

Sugar & creamer, Pearlized, set ....$45.00 – 50.00

Index